DISCARDED

Living Lively

Living Lively

80 PLANT-BASED RECIPES
TO ACTIVATE YOUR POWER & FEED YOUR POTENTIAL

HAILE THOMAS

WM
WILLIAM MORROW
An Imprint of HarperCollinsPublishers

TO MY IMMIGRANT PARENTS,
CHARMAINE AND HUGH:
THANK YOU FOR YOUR SACRIFICES,
OUR DINNER DEBATES, YOUR UNCONDITIONAL LOVE,
AND FOR EXPOSING ME TO THE WORLD AND
MY ENDLESS POTENTIAL WITHIN IT. THANK YOU
FOR HELPING ME BECOME SOMEONE I LOVE.

AND TO MY LITTLE SISTER, NIA:
THANK YOU FOR BEING THE BEST PARTNER IN LIFE
THAT I COULD EVER WISH FOR. YOUR HEART IS
UNMATCHED; YOU ARE THE SUNSHINE OF OUR LIVES.

IT IS IMPOSSIBLE TO PUT IN WORDS
HOW MUCH I LOVE AND APPRECIATE YOU ALL.

Contents

Introduction

I've probably identified with the term "foodie" since before I was even a fully developed fetus . . . and that's barely an exaggeration. Coming from two very Jamaican parents, I know my pregnant mom was going to all of her favorite authentic Jamaican spots in Dallas, my birthplace, and cooking up a storm— most likely making curry shrimp. And, by default, I was getting a taste. This deeply rooted heritage plays a huge part in my love and obsession with food and somewhat unusual (to Americans—no shade) ingredients. I was never a chicken nugget, Tater Tot, mac 'n' cheese kind of kid (weird flex, I know), and much preferred food slathered in spices like curry and jerk ordered from the "adult" menu. I absolutely despised the kids' menu and was kind of offended by it. Okay, I'll admit, I was a little bit of a food snob. But who could blame mini-me? I mean, my favorite activities at age eight were:

* Going to food festivals
* Eating out at restaurants
* Watching endless episodes of the old-school Japanese *Iron Chef*
* Cooking alongside my mom and little sister, Nia
* Reading fairy tales
* And I also did a little acting on the side . . . but we don't talk about that (my grade-school performance as Toto in *The Wizard of Oz* deserved an *Oscar*, okay?!).

While working as a kitchen apprentice to my mom (mostly stirring and observing until I was old enough to reach the stove without a step stool) I was inspired by her effortless creativity and how she moved about the kitchen in such a deliberate and intentional way. It looked like fun, and I could feel the love she infused into every dish. From this foundation, my interest in food grew stronger as I got older and slowly but surely earned more freedom in the kitchen, continuing to watch my mom, ask questions, and mimic her knife skills, the way she handled hot pots, or how she "eyeballed" when seasoning dishes. Eventually, I earned her trust to create whatever I could dream up. Food just always brought me great happiness. And it still does!

DESTINY IN A DIAGNOSIS

Jump into this mental time machine with me. . . . Let's rewind to 2009, the first year of President Barack Obama's first term, the year of the viral "David after dentist" video, and the year that laid the foundation for the rest of my life. Looking back on this year with my nostalgia glasses on, I can see how bittersweet life is—how brilliant, amazing things can come out of something that at first seems totally horrible.

It was the usual sweltering hot summer in Tucson, Arizona; the concrete literally radiated heat. Everything did. It was so hot that cooking eggs on the sidewalk could be perceived as a *logical* idea. It was so hot that putting on your seatbelt and accidentally touching the metal might result in third-degree burns (if you know, you know). I had just finished the third grade and was so happy to get a break from my dreaded times tables and to spend my precious days relaxing, swimming, playing, cooking, and blissfully stuffing my face—at all of the summertime food festivals, of course.

One summer day stands out, though. The air was heavy (and hot) in the car as we drove to my dad's doctor appointment. I hated going to the doctor, and I always believed that only horrible things happened at the office. I vividly remember pestering my parents during the drive, asking in my tiny (and to be honest, probably cringey) voice if my dad was going to be okay. They didn't know, and told me we were going to find out some results.

That shut me up, but my mind was racing . . . only bad things happen at the doctor's, I believed. My memories are hazy on the actual appointment, but

I do remember us all sitting in the car after his checkup, my mom reading off a terrifying list of side effects associated with the medicine my dad was prescribed. "May cause internal bleeding, weight gain, swelling of legs and ankles, diarrhea, skin rash, and itching . . ." she read aloud. My heart suddenly housed a thousand caged butterflies, battering against my chest. Endless thoughts were flying in and out of my mind as I internalized what I had just heard. Why would my dad take medicine that would cause problems that he didn't already have? I thought the doctor wanted to help him get better. I didn't understand what type 2 diabetes was at that point, but I did know something was very wrong with what the doctor had prescribed for him as a way to "get better."

That day passed, I got distracted, and my focus on it faded soon enough, as most things do for little kids. But I took notice when my mom increased our trips to the library and spent hours in Barnes & Noble, leaving with a stack of health-focused books. Even at home, she seemed to be doing some pretty intense research, with a specific focus on food.

At dinner my mom started to share what she was learning about nutrition. "You know you don't have to take this medication, Hugh . . ." she would announce. This piqued my interest, as anything about food did. And if we could stop our dad from taking this horrible medication, I wanted to be a part of the process.

Soon enough, I found myself completely invested in learning every and anything I could about this incredibly deep and multidimensional world of food. Together as a family, we watched popular health documentaries like *Forks Over Knives, Food, Inc.,* and *Fat, Sick & Nearly Dead.* If we weren't watching something, we were reading or trying new healthy recipes in the kitchen. Very quickly, food became much more than a form of happiness and comfort defined by flavor and seasonings; we became obsessed with learning about empty calories, incomprehensible food labels, strange processed food products, factory farming, childhood obesity, seasonal organic foods, healthy fats, plant proteins, and—most important—the opportunity we had to save my dad from his diagnosis without the use of medication.

And here's the best news ever! Eventually, we were able to do just that. Within a year we completely reversed his type 2 diabetes after putting in consistent effort to create lasting healthy lifestyle and eating habits.

With this incredible success, I became a bubbling pot of information, pun intended (keep reading—it won't be the last of its kind), and it was growing increasingly hard for me to hold back all that I learned.

Just imagine—you're chilling, eating some potato chips with not a care in the world, and then a nine-year-old kid with the mousiest little voice starts yelling at you to put your potato chips down because "you could die!!" I can't decide whether that is frightening, annoying, or both. Okay, it's probably both. I would legit roll up on my friends, upset with their food choices, and unintentionally scare them away. And to be real with y'all, if I were on the receiving end of that kind of conversation, I would run away, too! My intentions were the definition of pure. I just didn't want my friends to get sick because of what they ate . . . the way my dad had. But clearly, I didn't know how to translate these feelings and my newfound knowledge into positive communication. (But can we please cut young Haile some slack?? She's only nine!)

Frustrated with my many failed attempts to spread health "awareness" to my peers, I looked to my mom for advice. I just wanted to help other kids understand how amazing nourishing food is, and how delicious it can be! I wanted them to know that they didn't have to be bystanders in their lives . . . that they could have an active role in their health. I felt in my heart and soul that every young person deserved to be fully educated about what they put into their bodies. Because when we are informed, we're no longer victims of our actions and ignorance, but in the driver's seat.

The lack of food and nutrition education in my community and all around the country made me upset, because I knew that knowledge and awareness alone could change and impact so many lives. Sharing my frustrations and hopes with my mom helped me work things out. She took me seriously (thankfully!), and we discussed ways that I could potentially direct all of this passion into something positive and productive. *Side note: Contrary to popular belief, parents can make for really dope partners—if they don't downplay the awareness, intelligence, and passion of young people!*

One of our ideas was for me to join an advisory board or volunteer with a health-focused nonprofit. Luckily, it wasn't too hard to find organizations doing great work—there were quite a few. But one stood out the most: the Alliance for a Healthier Generation, with the goal of combating childhood obesity through school programs, partnerships, and a shiny and golden youth advisory board. I was so incredibly excited about this opportunity and immediately applied to join the board. After months of interviews and conversations with some of the Alliance staff, I discovered via a surprise Skype call that I was selected to represent the youth advisory board for the state of Arizona! During my four-year term with the Alliance I traveled to health advocacy training sessions all around the country, learned more about this country's childhood obesity crisis, and got a taste of the potential my activism had to make a greater impact.

As a result of my journey and budding passion, I was presented with incredible opportunities to speak and share my thoughts and opinions with corporate and nonprofit leaders focused on food and health, as well as with adults and young people all over the country. I didn't even know I was "good" at speaking . . . but the fearlessness and courage intrinsically linked to being a kid had me believe I could do it. There was something truly magical that happened when I was on stage, speaking from the heart. I had such a deep love for talking about how important it is for young people to become leaders in their lives through personal wellness . . . and because of that, people listened. By age ten I'd finished my first major speech at the Partnership for a Healthier America Summit and met and spoke with First Lady Michelle Obama for the first of six times. I know, I can't believe it either!! And did a TEDx talk in Vancouver, Canada. You have no idea how blown away I was. If my first official year of activism was this amazing and impactful, how incredible would the future be?

HOW WHAT WE CONSUME INFLUENCES EVERYTHING

The past ten-plus years of consistent participation in the wellness world has honestly been a blessing. At a young age, I secured my seat at the table, and that automatically caused people to take notice and regard my voice and contribution to the conversation as unique and valued. As a young person with an opinion and vision outside of herself who could also effectively communicate that vision to adults, I was considered an anomaly for a long time. And, I genuinely wanted to help make the world a healthier place. But honestly, I can't fully attribute all of my success to just those qualities.

Finding a purpose, understanding and deconstructing my fears, discovering the value of always speaking my truth, making an impact in communities that mean a lot to me, experiencing incredible "pinch me" moments each year, and now this book (!!!)—these things are the direct result of my life experiences and influences.

We are born consumers. From day one, everything we hear, see, touch, and feel is internalized and digested—mentally and physically. Over time, we unconsciously become these things. We internalize the views and opinions of our friends and family, the way people treat us out in the world, and how we react to that treatment, including characters on TV and in other media that constantly portray and perpetuate gender, race, and socioeconomic stereotypes. Then there's the overwhelming amount of bad news we are exposed to, the often unattainable beauty and lifestyle "goals" society shows us, the pressure to win (who decided life was a game?), and the idea that winning means fame, money, owning expensive things, and external validation. We also can't forget the degrading and dehumanizing ways some cultures, countries, and communities are displayed in the media and by irresponsible leaders . . . the list goes on and on. Influences like these can lead us to become unhappy, unfulfilled, scared of our own power, and unenthusiastic about life. Which sucks, because we should all know we have the power to Live Lively in some capacity—regardless of circumstances in our past or present.

While we can't fully control who's in our lives, we can recognize who does and does not impact us in healthy and nourishing ways. This helps us cultivate and nurture relationships with the humans that *do* leave us energized, curious, excited, and enticed by the world and our potential . . . with no cap on who we're destined to be. For me, it was hearing loving and encouraging words from my family and learning how important it was to echo and truly believe these words that gave me courage. It was learning how important it is to be a productive conspiracy theorist—questioning all things from the inside out to gain real understanding . . . not to become famous on Reddit (no offense if you've become famous off of Reddit conspiracy theory threads). And even taking up the challenge to question my own thoughts and actions with patience and love.

This comfort with asking questions is what made my family look into food as a form of medicine. It's what's allowed me to confront the way the traditional education system has conditioned us to view intelligence, discovering that it's not defined by standardized test results but by our own ability to expand our minds beyond that system. Asking questions that may never have an easy answer, like, "Um, why are we here?" (still working on that one, BTW).

But while I was growing and expanding my mind, I was also dealing with identity-confronting experiences—like when I was five years old and two little girls at my neighborhood park told me I couldn't play with them because I didn't have blond hair and blue eyes like they did. That experience, while painful and confusing, presented the opportunity for a valuable conversation and lesson about how others might see me, and holding my own self-worth beyond their biases and misconceptions. I learned pretty early on that I should try my best to not let others set the standard for how I see and value myself. Sitting down with my parents and listening to the incredible and otherworldly accomplishments of my ancestors unlocked the historically powerful and simultaneously painful privilege of brown skin, opening up an internal and external dialogue on what my race inextricably defines for me. I had the opportunity to either love or hate the skin I'm in . . . and luckily, with all the positive and empowering examples of confident and self-loving BIPOC around me, I am constantly encouraged to continue to develop a positive and empowering perspective of myself, no matter what.

My experiences have reinforced for me that I am more than enough, and that my skin color and others' perception of it shouldn't—and doesn't—define who I am or what I am capable of. I learned that good things will come my way if I stay true, and that I should express myself in all directions with authenticity—nothing less, and that even the word *impossible* says *I'm possible* (a saying my dad, for some reason, pretends he made up). But it's not always as simple as that. Both inside and outside of the cocoons of our homes and the people who love us, we can pick up mind-sets and perceptions that make us self-critical, negative, and insecure.

'Cause we're all just learning how to figure it out from humans who are still figuring it out. And as young people, we are constantly subjected to the influences of others, while few of us are presented with the choice to build our own foundations of self. I mean, even our very first words were not an act of choice, but of mimicry. So, who are we, really, until we get the opportunity to decide that for ourselves?

The good thing is that, like Play-Doh, we can be molded and deconstructed over and over again. We can decide how our experiences will impact our lives. There's so much power in saying, *"I'm going to redefine myself. I'm going to do what I can to strengthen the positive characteristics and actions that I believe will improve my life and the way I interact with the world around me."*

And just like that, who we are becomes an endlessly emerging possibility. The journey isn't guaranteed to be easy, but we are entirely capable of reconstructing the influences in our lives so that we can unleash our highest potential to grow and do anything. By tapping into this hidden power of constant opportunity to shift and change, we can become the architects of our lives, no matter how set in our ways we may think we are. And we can use our relationship with food as a strong foundation for fueling this reconstruction as well. On the surface, our relationship with food can be seen as defined by its necessity, but the way we perceive nourishing ourselves and our bodies is a product of societal influence, which can be more complicated than simply fulfilling nutritional needs. Especially during the transition from kid to young adult, seeing our bodies change and mature as we grow can be a time where we begin to project societal expectations onto ourselves and our bodies, creating potential for destructive comparison, food-related anxiety, dieting, and eating disorders. Through this lens, our relationships with food are built upon a disconnection from and objectification of our bodies. So instead of recognizing the body-mind connection as a core part of who we are (that needs to be nurtured), we try to exercise control over how we look and how others see us through our eating habits. For example, instead of feeling "imperfect" based on how we look and the standards projected onto us, we can ask ourselves if we really *feel* comfortable in our bodies, no matter what we *think* we look like. If we genuinely feel unhealthy, we can take action to nourish our bodies. And if we feel healthy, we should celebrate that and move on! When we get real with ourselves, we start to nourish the forever changing, beautiful energy that flows through us, and that helps us focus on improving other aspects of our lives.

PLOT TWIST: THIS BOOK IS ABOUT *YOU*

If you didn't know or guess by now, this isn't just a cookbook—it's an interactive book to encourage self-reflection, self-love, and self-empowerment! It's got a lot to do with self . . . and that ain't selfish! As a certified bibliophile, I love being able to take notes and reflect or comment on what I'm reading, especially if I feel as though it's stirring up something and I need an outlet to put these thoughts and feelings out into the universe and into action. So, welcome to your most unlikely journal! A place where food stains and deep thoughts can coexist! Who would've thought? Now, let's test this thing out. . . .

As the first task on the job as your own life's architect, go ahead and list the influences in your life that you feel may have unintentionally shaped your life/views/opinions/outlook (can be positive, negative, or neutral) and what you hope to deconstruct.

BIGGEST LIFE SHAPERS:

....

....

....

....

....

....

WHAT'S UP FOR DECONSTRUCTION?

....

....

....

....

....

....

....

WHAT IT MEANS TO FUEL OUR FUTURE

Maybe you've never taken the time to identify or think about all of the incredibly diverse influences that have created who you are, or perhaps you're well aware of what has brought you to your current state. Wherever you are in this journey, I'm already ridiculously proud of you. For taking a chance on this book, and for taking a chance on you and your forever-evolving self.

The thing about the future is that it exists only in our minds. The only tangible moment in life is now . . . oh, kidding, I mean *now*. Oh, that passed, too . . . hold up. *NOW.* You get what I mean! The future and present are basically one and the same. Now just happened, and that now just passed, and the now I was looking forward to is, well, now. My brain hurts a little, but we're just stretching these mental muscles.

With a clear understanding of the impermanence of time, and that we are literally time expressed as living, breathing lil cuties . . . we can decide that we'll use each moment to empower ourselves. And this certainly does not mean being happy 24/7 or being perfectly confident and fearless in all facets of our lives. But rather, recognizing the power each moment has to transform into something valuable—using all experiences as tools for growth. Keeping ourselves in mind as we move through life and trying our best to move in an upward direction with our personal wellness   which includes physical, mental, and environmental care. Creating a voice in your head that's like your best friend in the corner—the one who's always cheering you on and somehow always has the best advice.

So, don't be so hard on yourself. Some of our biggest "flaws" have been picked up, not selected. And when we are aware of this, we then have the choice to keep them around or work on kicking them to the curb. With no class or tutorial on being a functional human, we have a pretty cool opportunity to become our own teachers, customizing and evolving that learning experience as we ourselves experience life and evolve.

But seriously, though, what would happen if we became our own teacher? Our biggest supporter? Our own healer and hero, turning growing pains into growing gains? What would happen if we fueled our *now* and *next* by being aware of who we are and who we want to be, and what impacts these things?

As you go through this book, keep your power in mind. Connect to and see yourself in the stories of each of the five absolutely incredible young women featured in the 7 Points of Power as a source of inspiration. Look to the fabulously flavorful and nourishing recipes in this book and the intentional Power Noms (page 259) as a source of body fuel.

Energy never dies, but it transforms. So, as you read on, ask yourself, what imbalances do you feel within that can be transformed through a change of thought, an action, meal, or opening up and asking for help? Connect to this book in whatever way feels good to you. There is no right or wrong way to use it!

LIVING LIVELY—IT'S A LIFESTYLE

Sometimes, I wonder if enough of me lies outside of what I do. Who am I without this work? And to be honest, I don't entirely know. In certain scenarios throughout my life, I have shrunk and expanded in order to fit the environment. Not because I was fake, but because I was confused. Maybe you can relate to this. Who am I without my friends, family, hobbies, school, job, biggest dream? I still have my moments when I return to mimicking or conforming. But I've made peace with it, because who I am is always shifting and changing. And we will never know who we fully are, anyway—we change every day.

But that isn't depressing; it's freeing. It allows us to be anyone, capable of doing anything.

Living Lively is not about being perfect and understanding the formula to life inside and out. To be entirely honest with you, I wrote most of this book in the midst of my crusty-looking, hot-mess bedroom, which I tend to neglect when I get busy. And juggling the whole new territory of book writing plus other projects brought up a lot of internal challenges along the way. But I've learned so much about myself and my strength through it all. I've discovered that Living Lively is really about being *okay* with the journey and nurturing all the greatness that already exists within—handling new challenges with love, grace, and introspection.

It's caring for yourself along the way, being present as much as possible, indulging in whatever happiness looks like for you, and fully feeling, then reflecting on, sadness, jealousy, anger, joy, and so on. Living Lively is just *being*—with love for all you are, can, and will be, without judging yourself or the process. And with letting the weight of judgment from others roll off your shoulders. Working on letting go of limiting beliefs and mind-sets, limiting people, limiting foods and habits, and limiting environments in the ways you can.

Trust yourself, you've got this—and it's time to start your adventure.

I personally find intention setting to be one of the biggest positive practices in my life. Identifying and expressing what you hope to give to and receive from the world is one of the most beautiful and powerful things we can do for ourselves.

So, what do you hope to get out of this book? How will you Live Lively? Who do you want to be? What do you want to do? Where do you want to be, mentally and physically? What do you hope to improve after reading this book? What do you hope to love and enjoy about yourself just a little bit more? What do you want to celebrate about you? Exercise your power to define yourself and hold yourself accountable. This is all about you, and it's amazing (not selfish or narcissistic!). Dig in and dig deep. This is your garden, plant those seeds!!

My intentions as I read this book

....

....

....

....

....

....

....

....

WELCOME TO YOUR PERSONAL POWER

I'm so incredibly excited to share with you what I lovingly call the "7 Points of Power"! During this process of growing up and facing internal and external challenges, I've recognized different elements that have played a huge role (whether I'm aware of it or not) in shaping my daily experience as a human. They are some of the foundational elements of our lives, and they hold incredible opportunities for us to thrive if we reimagine and redefine them:

- * Wellness
- * Thoughts and Mind-Set
- * Relationships
- * Social Media and Societal Influences

- * Education
- * World Perspective
- * Creativity and Community

Through reimagining and redefining these points of power in my life, I've found ways to finally let go of wanting to be liked by everyone, truly love and appreciate my body, and be content with my imperfectly perfect life journey—unlocking genuine happiness and freedom that has allowed me to ebb and flow in order to learn and grow. My biggest hope and intention is that through the advice, stories, and experiences shared in these 7 Points of Power, this book can become something like a "Human 101" guide or "big sister" that you can lean on if you ever forget just how amazing you are.

WHY OUR POWER MATTERS

One of the things that I've learned about life (so far—I'm just getting started up in here) that has really stuck with me is that our habits, mind-set, relationships, interests, and perceptions are what make us who we are. And for most of our lives, these elements have come together unconsciously. As little kids, we built our perception of ourselves and our potential off of the examples of confidence and potential we had access to. We shaped our world view based on how our family, friends, and community saw it. We learned to limit ourselves based on what we were told were our limits. We learned how to love ourselves (or not love ourselves) based on the examples around us . . . and the list goes on and on. Who we are is influence-based! And the big lesson is that with awareness of this fact, we can become our own influencers (minus the brand deals).

I want this reading experience and the 7 Points of Power to empower you to go beyond what you might believe is possible, to dig deeper, treat yourself with kindness, and redefine what your world looks like. As you read through the 7POP, you'll also meet five young and amazing humans who share their journeys and wisdom on the points of power that they've been able to leverage to create a lively life. And just like the journeys and stories of these women, I want you to remember that the 7 Points of Power are multidimensional, interconnected, and probably have hundreds of micro power points within them.

So, keep your mind open and remember that this is your book! You have the freedom to dig in and find out what each point means to you and how these concepts might fit into your life. My realizations and those of these five women may or may not fully resonate with your life, but they could spark the start of a journey to figure it out. You never know what stories or ideas just might push you that much closer to an important breakthrough!

And you know what? I challenge you to challenge this book and all of the ideas shared—because just like you, I'm always growing up and always learning more. And growing usually requires handling challenges, being uncomfortable, not knowing everything, and tapping into curiosity. This possibility to expand who we are and what we know is a constant reminder of just how cool it is to be a human that's always changing. Look at all that potential!! It's stunning.

BEFORE YOU GET STARTED!
(OPTIONAL, BUT HIGHLY RECOMMENDED)

On the next page you can do a little speed reflecting! Before diving into the 7 Points of Power, think about what each one means to you in your own life. What points of power do you sense some imbalance within and especially want to nourish? Which ones do you already feel strongest in, and why. Clear your mind and enter the 7POP with *you* in mind. Mindfulness, honesty, and vulnerability with yourself is sometimes the deepest, sweetest, and simplest solution to overcoming obstacles and truly determining how you want to Live Lively.

My 7 points of power are:

1. Wellness: ....
....

2. Thoughts and Mind-Set: ....
....

3. Relationships: ....
....

4. Social Media and Societal Influences: ....
....

5. Education: ....
....

6. World Perspective: ....
....

7. Creativity and Community: ....
....

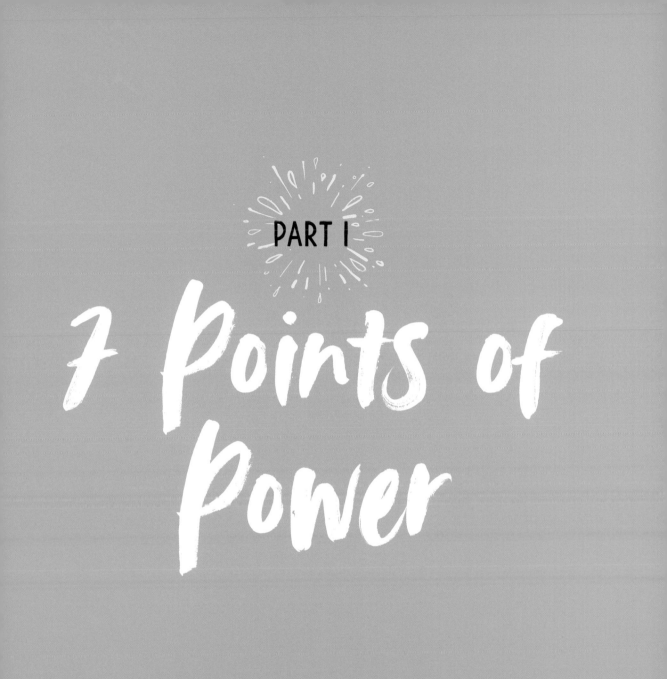

PART I

7 Points of Power

POP 1
Wellness

Wellness is multidimensional by nature and, therefore, can get super bogged down and confusing. So to make this a little easier, let's break wellness down! There are typically seven parts to it that overlap to create overall well-being.

SPIRITUAL WELLNESS
EMOTIONAL/MENTAL WELLNESS
PHYSICAL WELLNESS
INTELLECTUAL WELLNESS
ENVIRONMENTAL WELLNESS
SOCIAL WELLNESS
FINANCIAL WELLNESS

As you can see, most of these seven parts to wellness are represented in the 7 Points of Power, indicating that these are all interconnected and help us create all-around health and well-being. While we're not going to deep dive into all of them (I'm still trying to figure out how to build credit, so you'll have to look somewhere else for tips on finances, *ha-ha*), I want you to think about each one and how they are represented and defined in your life. Our perception of these aspects of wellness is just the beginning of creating a positive relationship with our well-being. When we determine for ourselves what wellness does and does not represent, we're building the road map to unlocking our personal power.

When we have a vision of what wellness looks like, we can take intentional actions to help achieve those goals. Zooming out so we can zoom in! So, for example, this is how I see wellness as a whole:

WELLNESS IS:

* Celebrating where we are in our health journeys
* Seeing every day as a new beginning and opportunity to do good for ourselves
* Letting go of shame in our journeys
* Striving to create healthy and sustainable habits
* Moving and eating in ways that we love and make our bodies feel good
* Listening to our bodies, not diet culture, and acting accordingly
* Engaging in positive self-talk
* Finding space for exploration and self-discovery
* Fueling our bodies with delicious, real foods as much as possible
* Putting joy first (prioritizing the things that make us happy)
* Being vulnerable and listening to our inner voice

WELLNESS ISN'T:

* Stressing over what to eat
* Judging ourselves heavily for every "bad" decision or misstep we make
* Judging our bodies
* Feeling depressed or sad about what we are eating for the sake of "health"
* Pushing our bodies in unhealthy ways to look a certain way or to meet a certain standard
* Feeling it necessary to have a particular body type
* Comparing ourselves to people in real life and on social media and their bodies, habits, or lifestyle
* Putting unrealistic or harsh expectations on our wellness journeys

SO, WHAT DO YOU DEFINE WELLNESS AS?

IF YOU WANT, YOU CAN WRITE A LIL SOMETHING BELOW:

For me, wellness is:

With clearly defined ideas of what wellness means to us, we can dive into each aspect of it with intention and clarity. So keep these definitions in mind as you read through the related points of power! Though each aspect of wellness is important in its own way, physical and intellectual wellness are some of the most important to focus on as foundations. Without physical and intellectual wellness, we don't have the energy to cultivate health and healthy mind-sets in other aspects of our lives. So for your action plan for our first point of power, let's dig into the importance of nurturing these forms of wellness—because how we move and stretch our bodies and minds shapes the way in which we show up in our world.

LET'S GET PHYSICAL

Getting rest, eating nourishing foods, learning from experience, moving our bodies, exposing ourselves to new ideas, consistently taking care of our skin— these are all self-care activities that nurture physical and intellectual wellness. It's a balancing act of prioritizing and actively engaging in these things that help us feel cared for from the inside out, fostering optimal health and functioning. But where to start?

This feels like one of the biggest unanswered questions in the universe: Does a school-life or work-life balance even *exist*?? Okay, maybe it's not the biggest unanswered question in the universe—but it sure can feel like it. At one point or another, we are bound to feel overwhelmed by the looming responsibility of taking care of ourselves while still focusing on work and school. Is it possible to keep up with ourselves and the world? In the past year, I've asked myself this question a lot and struggled with really prioritizing my physical wellness. If nothing else, I was pretty consistent with keeping my food choices healthful— but even then, I felt disconnected, increasingly dealing with acne, unsure of what was causing it. And the other elements of wellness? We don't know her. They were completely absent from my day to day. I started to feel drained and

distant from myself and my passions. And that really scared me. How could I feel so disconnected from the things I knew I loved? But the truth is, when you don't put energy into yourself, you're bound to feel unbalanced—no matter what you're doing. I was letting my work life dominate my *entire* life, and it was taking a significant toll on my physical and mental wellness. It made it harder for me to give anything 100 percent.

By moving through each day unconsciously, without my own well-being in mind, I became convinced that the needs, deadlines, and expectations of others were far more important than my own. I internalized this so much that it felt like a fact. There just wasn't enough time in the world to make *myself* a priority. (Spoiler alert: There is always enough time for *you*. Nothing is more important than *you time*.) I was too ashamed to let anyone know I was struggling because I felt like the biggest hypocrite. I knew what I should have been doing and still felt like I had no choice or time. But—plot twist—there is always something we can do. I was just so overwhelmed by everything I had to, and wanted to, do that I chose to be powerless. Responsibility weighing heavy on my shoulders, I was stuck in a revolving door of unproductive thoughts and was beating myself up for all the things I failed to do for my self-care. This is when I finally understood the importance of self-care on a deeper level. It's not just some cute thing where you throw a face mask on or read a book over the weekend. It is something we must prioritize in one way or another every. single. day. Putting consistent effort toward caring for ourselves is key. Doing so as we go through life equips us with the physical and mental strength to take on challenges (with our best foot forward) as they come instead of being so depleted that any bump in the road takes all our energy. Daily self-care helps prevent negative thoughts from being enforced so often that they become our default. It helps shield our bodies and minds from being constantly exhausted by internal and external stressors.

I knew I needed to make a massive change, or I would continue to lose my zest for life. How could I possibly do or expect better for myself if I was approaching it all with so much negativity? I had to reshape my relationship with self-care and other priorities completely. It wasn't just being overwhelmed that was hindering me, but the way I was communicating with myself. So I sat down and analyzed my personal routine, quickly realizing I didn't actually *have* one anymore. I would wake up and just start doing the things I needed to work on. I was losing myself because I wasn't creating space *for* myself. I needed a way to focus each day and put *well-being and gratitude* at the center, so I could stay centered. I searched all over the Internet for "remixed to-do lists" or "positive to-do lists," and I couldn't find anything. So I made my own.

This tool I'm sharing with you is called a Grateful to Prioritize Today (GTPT) list, and it has truly changed my life inside and out. I created it so that I could intentionally structure and create awareness around the things I do personally and professionally. It has made taking care of myself and my obligations feel manageable. And I started to pay attention to how I felt in my body, making sure it genuinely felt good. Because this list puts self-care, mental wellness, and mindfulness at the center of every day—it creates a ripple effect! The more we feel the happiness, pride, and rejuvenation that come from eating well, moving our bodies, and being intellectually engaged, the more we want to keep it up. I feel motivated and proud of myself because I know I put my wellness first and approach my day with the best energy. The secret sauce in the GTPT list is that self-care, positivity, and awareness are the foundations of it. My daily lists remind me of what is essential. They remind me to reflect often. And that the best I can do is be present and accepting of whatever is happening internally and externally, and taking action accordingly.

ACTION PLAN

Try making your own GTPT list! The great thing about it is that it's highly customizable, so you can add whatever you need to nourish yourself for the day! Fill this out with intention. It doesn't have to be overwhelming; focus on all the little things that add up to a more loving, positive, and proactive you. Oh, and decorate and draw all over this space if you want to! I recommend you fill your list out the night before a new day. That's what I do! *Have fun with it!*

Things I'm grateful to prioritize today

DATE: /   /

AOD (AFFIRMATION OF THE DAY): WRITE A PHRASE HERE THAT YOU LOVE OR RESONATE WITH AND WILL FOCUS ON FOR THE DAY:

....

....

....

Today I want to feel (for each item, detail what actions you'll take to feel that way):

....

....

....

....

 I Love You List/AM (self-care things you'd like to do for yourself in the morning):

....

....

....

....

I Love You List/PM (same as above—the nighttime version):

....

....

....

....

....

Growing My Dreams List (This is where traditional "to-do" items go! But write them as actions that need to take place to build your dreams and your best life. Organize them by category—such as school, personal, and creative. . . .):

....

....

....

....

....

....

....

....

....

....

Day in Review

Today my body felt good when I:

....

....

....

....

Today I took care of my health/happiness by eating or doing:

....

....

....

....

My energy today was:

....

....

....

....

IF YOU'D LIKE TO USE THE GTPT LIST EVERY DAY, HEAD TO THIS LINK TO DOWNLOAD THE TEMPLATE :)

WWW.HAILEVTHOMAS.COM/GTPTLIST

Not ready to try out the GTPT list yet? Just remember that micro moments of awareness can make a massive difference, too. Try placing awareness onto your body after meals or physical activity and see what you discover. Keep a journal to track how you feel and how your body reacts. Finished reading something that was thought provoking? Reflect on what you learned and spend a few minutes thinking about how you could apply it to your life. Step out of your comfort zone now and then. Ask yourself how you feel pre and post. Just take a moment to be with your body and mind.

It's time
.to blossom.

Thoughts and Mind-Set

Our thoughts and the way we see ourselves set the stage for how we treat ourselves on a daily basis. When we feel unimportant, lost, or disconnected from our reason for being in this world, we speak to and treat ourselves as if we don't matter. This can cause depression, anxiety, and indifference toward life. But the thing is, if you've experienced these feelings based on certain external circumstances or environments, and have developed negative thought patterns and mind-sets, know that (a) it's okay and (b) you have the power to change, if not the circumstance or environment itself, definitely your perspective and reaction to it.

How, exactly? Of course, just saying "be positive!" is so clichéd and way easier said than done. I don't know about you, but I am beyond tired of surface-level positivity advice and tips. Being positive often takes self-discovery and dedication that go far beyond simply acknowledging our challenges or reading a positive quote on a social media post. In my experience, it takes dismantling the disempowering lies we've absorbed (from media, friends, family, teachers) and repeated to ourselves over time. It takes identifying those root causes, patience, love, and self-compassion in order to heal. But that journey is worth it more than anything in the world and opens us up to start to unlock the ability to truly Live Lively.

Okay, now this all might sound good, but it can be overwhelming to think about reprogramming our brain, our constant internal chatter, and our outlook on life. But don't worry, I gotchu. :) Just remember, this mental strengthening and evolution come in waves and stages—through both predictable and unexpected progressions. Once we open ourselves up to learn and grow, we suddenly start to notice that the things going on in our lives aren't happening to hurt us but are happening to teach us something important. The difference is whether or not we're present and tuned into ourselves enough to be able to see the lesson.

Things to remember when you need to shift your thoughts or mind-set:

YOUR CHOICES BELONG TO YOU!

You can do anything you truly set your mind to, and ultimately your happiness is what's important. Yes, it's important to listen to the advice of those who love you or care about your well-being and future. But sometimes advice is just someone else's fear and doubt projected onto you, and it causes you to lose confidence and sight of what could be your actual life path. Of course, if someone advises you to stay away from obviously dangerous things like drugs, irresponsible drinking, putting yourself in true harm's way, and so on, you should listen to them. But if a person's input is causing you to question or second-guess your abilities or put a pause on your dreams, or someone is pressuring you to get a "regular" job, study something "useful," or stay in your lane, I want you to ask yourself, *What personal fears may they be projecting onto me, and should I internalize this?* By answering these questions, we separate their fears from our own. Maybe it's their or our own anxiety, past experiences and failures, vulnerability, and so on that are really driving the fear, rather than an actual threat to our lives.

If you're not doing, pursuing, or dreaming of something that brings you joy, who are you doing it for? Why? And what are you afraid of? Be honest with yourself. Is it judgment? Embarrassment? Fear of failure or disappointment?

Lack of trust in yourself? If it is any or all of these things, *it's okay!!* Emotions are human. It's okay and perfectly normal to be afraid of dreaming big or doing the unexpected. But getting to the root of that fear helps us get to know ourselves and our true potential. Once we can recognize the root of our fear, we can look at any experiences or influences that have made us believe it is valid. Challenge the root cause and determine what changes you can make in your thoughts and actions to dismantle that fear-inducing belief.

CREATE MINI MENTAL CELEBRATIONS!

Every. single. time. you are kind to yourself, handle a situation with emotional maturity, take a moment to appreciate the now and be present, or act purely out of your own motivations or follow what brings you joy and fulfillment, celebrate it! Do not miss these opportunities to show yourself love and pride.

For years I kept myself from feeling real pride because I cared too much about what people thought of me. I was terrified of coming across as "intimidating," because peers and adults would constantly tell me that I was—solely based on what I do. And even in talking about myself and my work by necessity, I feared appearing like I was "bragging" when in reality I was just explaining my life! And I'd hear well-intended, maybe accidentally self-deprecating comments like "You're doing all this? What have I done with my life?," which made me so uncomfortable with being who I am because I didn't want others to put themselves down "because of me."

These experiences led me to minimize myself. I'd tell myself that the "real me" was not the international speaker and CEO . . . but just Haile at home scrolling on IG. I couldn't fathom fully being both parts of myself. I thought I would be too much. But after one particular incident in which my personal choices and values were questioned and compared to others, I realized that it was no longer worth my time or energy to shapeshift just so someone else could be comfortable. The way others interpret my existence is none of my business—can't please everyone, anyway!

Just like the sun, the world needs all of our light. Why would we deprive it of something so essential, prohibiting ourselves and fellow beings from blossoming? When we shine, it helps others feel comfortable in doing the same.

Not everyone will appreciate or be able to handle the radiance that oozes out of us when we are proud of and stand behind all we are—the work-in-progress pieces and the parts of us we adore and that others might celebrate or honor. *Always* remember that's their problem. Either they need to put on some SPF and accept our shine or head inside and out of our way. This confidence, this knowing your power . . . you are worth feeling this way.

WHATEVER YOUR MIND BELIEVES IS *TRUE*!

What you believe and what you put energy toward is what becomes your reality. So, if you believe you're too shy to stand up for yourself, or that your community and upbringing defines your potential, then it is true. But if you believe that despite your temporary shyness, no one should walk all over and disrespect you, or that your upbringing only adds to your strength and story, then you will be able to rise up and out of anything. Perspective is everything.

MONITOR, FILTER, AND FLIP THE NEGATIVE!

Even if aspects of our lives seem bad or unchangeable, we *can* change—from the inside out. Take, for example, the weight of white supremacy and white privilege that tell me that because of my skin color, I lack power. This may manifest as a systemic structure that I can't (yet) dismantle personally, but I *can* dismantle its mental effects on me, which come from messages like, "Everything is harder for me because of who I am," "I'm not beautiful because of the color of my skin or texture of my hair," "I have no power," "The country hates me

and is out to get me," "I will never be successful," "I'll never make it out of this situation," "I am my upbringing," or "I'm defined by the past and controlled by the present."

I actually *do* have power if I nurture my mind and monitor, filter, and flip the messages that come through it. Instead of perceiving my journey as difficult before even embarking on it, I can view myself as strong and brave for seeing and acknowledging systemic barriers, yet not attaching them to my potential. By using this awareness, my experiences, and my strength in the ways I can to stand up for justice, compassion, and equality in their micro and macro manifestations, I can create change in my local and global community, starting with myself. We can choose to view even the negatives in our lives with optimism when we express gratitude for the power we do hold. Try taking advantage of the challenge or situation at hand and see how it might be able to help you learn, grow, level up, or even inspire a solution.

LOVE ALL YOUR EMOTIONS!

Okay, so if you think I walk around smiling 24/7, please, please erase that image from your head. Sometimes I just wake up in a bad mood for no reason at all, or get overwhelmed and frustrated and worried and cry a ton. That does not make me mentally or emotionally weak. Caring for your mental health does not mean avoiding your humanity and forcing yourself to be happy all the time! Suppressing how you feel just for the sake of being "happy and positive" does not create freedom; it creates resistance. Fighting with your feelings and pushing them down, unresolved, can manifest as health issues, internal conflict, and actually bring into your life more negativity and unhappiness.

Whenever I am stressed out and fight it or just tell myself to "push past it" instead of slowing down, acknowledging those feelings, and working through them, I always end up feeling sick. Reprogramming myself to pause and analyze how I feel and redirect my thoughts and energy is still something I'm working on to this day. And I'm perfectly fine with that, because it's a process that takes certain experiences and time to reach healing. Placing pressure on myself to master my stress only adds to it.

The best way I've found so far to navigate emotions and stop them from controlling me is to disconnect myself from them, to experience and observe them but not embody them. Instead of saying or thinking "I'm upset," which is possessive and identifying, try "I'm feeling upset." This bases the emotion on your current experience, not your identity. You are not your emotions; you are just experiencing them in this moment in time. And if you're having trouble shaking a feeling, don't be afraid of asking for help and seeking a family member, friend, or medical professional that you trust. There is no shame in needing support to nurture your mind and heal your emotions. Your well-being is far more important than anyone's adverse opinion.

GRATITUDE IS A MUST!

The idea of gratitude can be overwhelming. On one hand, we can easily believe we have nothing to be grateful for when we place our values on objects, status, external validation, and tons of money or success. And on the other, we can find abundant things to be grateful for when we focus on the truly meaningful pieces of life—such as our beating hearts, the people in our lives, the sunset on a Tuesday, the ability to communicate, access to knowledge, the book (my book, *he-he*) in your hands, the feeling of grass tickling between your toes, your freedom of speech. Air! Clouds! Tacos! Your Instagram followers! Anything and everything. Think about just how special these things are and how good you feel while experiencing them. I know that when I talk with my family and friends I feel so engaged, understood, and cared for. This love and mutual attentiveness is a privilege to feel. I also frequently take time to be grateful for the strength of my body. It has carried me through life with such sturdiness that could easily be taken for granted. My good health is something worth celebrating every day.

Meet Lulu

LULU GAFFGA is the popular twenty-year-old German self-love and vegan advocate behind the Instagram account @LulusDreamTown and the podcast *Selbstverliebt mit Lulu* (*Self-Love with Lulu*). Her message of self-love, positivity, and developing compassionate relationships with ourselves has touched the lives of hundreds of thousands of people of all ages from all around the world.

I'm so thrilled to include some of the wisdom that Lulu shared with me as we discussed the importance of healthy relationships with ourselves. She was one of my first social media inspirations, and it has been beautiful witnessing her light and message grow year after year.

Haile: **Have you always had a positive relationship with yourself? How did you start this journey of self-love and self-empowerment and then sharing it with hundreds of thousands on social media?**

Lulu: I was always this happy child, always smiling and having fun. But when I was around ten years old, some people started telling me that I was "chubby" and things like that, and I was always the girl who was curvier than the others. I started disliking my body and myself more and more. And when I was thirteen, I started dieting, and my eating disorder started as well. I was hating myself so bad. Everything—my body, my life. But I think through that experience I started researching self-love, and it took me three years to come to a place where I was truly starting to love myself. And right now I'm really happy with the journey and how much I have achieved. While I had my eating disorder, I realized that I had to do something about it and save myself. I went to different therapists, but nothing really helped because I felt like they couldn't really relate to what I was going through. So I looked on Instagram and YouTube and found people sharing similar struggles, and I was inspired to do the same. I want to be this helpful person to someone else, because someone helped me, too.

Haile: What is your best advice for someone who wants to build a healthy relationship with themselves?

Lulu: I think this is a big topic, because everyone is different, but I would start with being your own best friend. No matter what kind of situation you're currently living in, think about how your best friend would take care of you, or what tips they would give you. They wouldn't be like, "Yeah, you suck"; they would be like, "You're great! Just the way you are!" Building a relationship through having a friendship with yourself is important. There are a lot of stereotypes that self-love is just for women, or that wanting to lose weight or put on makeup isn't self-love. So, we have to really have a positive mind-set about self-love before we even start it.

This may sound confusing, but I maintain my happiness because I kind of don't maintain it. If people tell me they're always happy, I don't really believe it. I just want us to stay human. It is human to be vulnerable or to have bad days or to cry. So, I maintain my happiness by truly accepting everything that will happen; when I

have a bad day, I will have a bad day. You have to truly accept yourself instead of trying to be this perfect something. People want to tell us that sadness is a bad thing, but having bad days here and there and truly feeling it and then letting go helps us move forward.

Haile: What does Living Lively mean to you?

Lulu: Truly being yourself, and growing, and just experiencing life with everything that happens no matter if it is positive or negative—and just being there. I take care of myself a lot more than I used to, so I try to listen to my gut and show myself more love instead of judging. Changing my mind-set is really what helps me the most.

SURPRISE!

PAUSE FOR A SECOND AND LIST 5 THINGS YOU'RE GRATEFUL FOR
THAT TYPICALLY GO UNNOTICED

I know I don't express it much, but I'm grateful for:

1. ....

....

....

2. ....

....

....

3. ....

....

....

4. ....

....

....

5. ....

....

....

ACTION PLAN

Take your mind on a date. If you wanted to win over your mind and make a good impression, what would you do? Sometimes when we think about loving ourselves more and being positive and mindful, it can become draining figuring out where to start. Here's a solo adventure you can have fun with!! So, treat your mind to a first date, as you'd call it. What activities and habits can you put in place to treat your mind right?

SOME DATE IDEAS:

* Zero distraction, mindful evenings watching the sunset
* Moments of gratitude right when you wake up and right before you go to bed
* Creating your own positive affirmations
* Following new people on social media who make you feel good and fill your heart and mind (and unfollowing anyone who doesn't)
* Trying something new or something that you're (unreasonably or emotionally) scared of

HOW ARE YOU GOING TO TREAT YOUR MIND?

....

....

....

....

....

....

Relationships

The relationships we have with ourselves and others are one of the biggest influences in our lives. Through these relationships we discover how to communicate, develop emotional skills, and learn how to express and perceive ourselves and the world. Disclaimer here. I am not in any way, shape, or form a "relationship expert." As of this writing I've been in, eh, about 0 romantic ones. So I can't speak to it all. But I can speak to the foundational elements of human connection that I've seen and felt deeply impact my life—in the ways I communicate with myself, friends, family, and strangers. Whatever the relationship, the people in our lives help shape who we are and influence how we act and think. Through relationships, our emotions and minds are unlocked, and we begin to unconsciously define what love, attention, validation, humor, compassion, anger, and so on mean to us—as well as how to express them.

BUILDING YOUR LIVELY GANG

CULTIVATING POWERFUL PARTNERSHIPS

While we can't control others, we can control (for the most part) who is a part of our inner circle and making the biggest impressions on us. Defining what we're looking to give, receive, and experience in our relationships with others helps us form connections with clarity, authenticity, and intention. By being aware of the impact the people closest to us can make on our moods and mind-sets, we can recognize that healthy and nourishing relationships are an incredibly important part of our self-care. Understanding the influence of re-lationships also helps *us* become more self-aware—we can work on becoming better friends, partners, and family members as well.

Write down a list of things you wish to give and receive in your relationships.

....

....

....

....

....

HERE'S SOME INSPIRATION:

* Support, trust, and honesty
* A safe space to be authentic
* Respectful boundaries
* Deep listening and genuine conversation
* Unconditional kindness and thoughtfulness
* Encouragement of physical and mental wellness

Based on your above answers, how do you define a healthy relationship?

....

....

....

....

....

Now let's zoom in. Remember, the quality in a relationship is based on how it feels, not how it looks on paper or how it is perceived by others. Think about your relationships with the top three most influential people in your life and how they make you feel:

Name: ....

How do I feel when I hang out with this person?

....

....

....

What do they do or say that makes me feel this way? (We love a rhyming question.)

....

....

....

....

Am I myself with this person?

....

....

Do they cause stress, drama, or feelings of insecurity?

....

....

....

....

What positive contributions do they make to my life?

....

....

....

....

Optional: How can I positively and productively address how I'm feeling in our relationship?

....

....

....

Name: ....

How do I feel when I hang out with this person?

....

....

....

....

What do they do or say that makes me feel this way?

....

....

....

Am I myself with this person?

....

....

....

Do they cause stress, drama, or feelings of insecurity?

....

....

What positive contributions do they make to my life?

....

....

....

Optional: How can I positively and productively address how I'm feeling in our relationship?

....

....

Name: ....

How do I feel when I hang out with this person?

....

....

What do they do or say that makes me feel this way?

....

....

....

Am I myself with this person?

....

....

....

Do they cause stress, drama, or feelings of insecurity?

....

....

....

What positive contributions do they make to my life?

....

....

....

Optional: How can I positively and productively address how I'm feeling in our relationship?

....

....

....

....

Regardless of the influence the people in our lives have on us, the way we see ourselves, the way we treat others and handle relationships don't have to be a product of what we've seen or experienced in the past. We all have a choice to maintain or disrupt who we are, our attitudes and ideas, and how we interact with the people we allow to be around us.

YOU ARE, LITERALLY, YOUR OWN BUILT-IN RIDE OR DIE
CULTIVATING A HEALTHY RELATIONSHIP WITH YOURSELF

Being open to investigating all that you know and feel about yourself is not cute work. It can be really confusing or upsetting and bring up shame, resentment, or judgment. You have to know that you are a work in progress, infinitely, and there's not one thing in the universe that isn't under construction. We are constantly changing, shrinking, expanding—wilting, blossoming. Accept who and where you are right now.

As for me, I'm embracing the journey of learning with openness and vulnerability. I know I will disappoint myself sometimes, that I'll miss some learning moments, and that even if I've been unkind to myself in the past, that *can* change. I'm not ashamed of what has made me who I am, and I am excited to see who I will help myself become.

When we embrace everything that has gotten us to today, we can have compassion for the journeys of others and build more meaningful relationships by connecting our humanity. Through this lens, there is really no such thing as "good and bad"—just experience and interpretation that everyone is working through. Embarking on a journey of acceptance and self-love helps the people in our lives become more comfortable with accepting and loving themselves, too. Our individual health always influences our inner circle. So for the well-being of ourselves and the people we love, embrace the way you might have judged your body, and thank the experience for showing you that you don't deserve to feel that way. Embrace the way you open your heart, even if it gets you hurt sometimes; thank your heart for showing you how deep it can be. Embrace the way you blamed yourself for being broken or weak; thank the experience for proving you're strong by bringing you to today. Embrace the way you may think your mental illness, disability, struggle, or circumstance defines you; thank your circumstances for helping you build resilience and strength, and then acknowledge that they do not define you and are only a part of your journey.

Write down some things you believe you are and aren't in control of changing—and accept them both. This acceptance might happen as easily as an exhale, or it might be something you have to gradually do over time. Either way, you're doing amazing. :)

I am in control of changing . . .

....

....

....

....

I am not in control of changing . . .

....

....

....

....

If you can't change something, you can perceive it differently, which makes all the difference. What's one positive thing you can take away from the things you can't control?

I can't change it, but I appreciate . . .

....

....

....

I can't change it, but I appreciate . . .

....

....

....

I can't change it, but I appreciate . . .

....

....

....

ACTION PLAN

#RelationshipGoals is, IMO, the cringiest hashtag on the Internet, but I think it can have a pretty practical application when it comes to envisioning what kind of relationship we hope to create with ourselves and the steps we can take to get there. So, what kind of relationship would you like to cultivate with yourself, how will it improve or transform your life, and how can you achieve that goal?

What defines your ideal relationship with yourself?

....

....

What are the top five ways you want to improve your relationship with yourself?

....

....

....

....

....

How can you achieve these goals? Who/what is needed?

....

....

....

....

How would this help you grow?

....

....

....

....

Social Media and Societal Influences

How does your "feed" feed you? We are a generation glued to the world in our pockets, enamored 24/7 of devices the size of our hands—with timelines, little red hearts, and Twitter wars as second nature. Social media has become the newest tool in which society influences and sets the tone. I am not one to say "social media is evil" or that it has ruined humanity, because (a) that isn't entirely true and (b) I'm addicted, and therefore defensive about it. I will admit that I'm definitely attached at the hip to my phone.

There are so many interesting and diverse things we can submerge ourselves into, all with the click of a button. We can avoid our responsibilities and fears, slowly fill our hearts, and boost our self-esteem with each validating "like" on our latest posts. We can feel a little less lonely with communities of people we may never meet. For most of us, media has both filled and deepened a void. Maybe that void is feeling unimportant offline and seeking importance online. Or being entertained because we don't believe our own lives are entertaining enough. It is a simultaneously sad and beautiful place, alternately very isolating and deeply connecting.

Whatever you may gain or lose from social media, you know there is incredible impact and influence from the platforms and people who create the culture. It is not AI or algorithms that have built meaningful communities and destructive, divisive comment sections—all of us have. We are the Internet. Which means it's up to us to use this platform consciously and change or create the environments we wish to have available to us and exist within.

I think there's this common idea in older generations that our phones are demonic and that they make us dumber, less attentive, distracted, desensitized, and aggressive. Now, this is all a possibility, depending on the people and spaces we participate in. But when we acknowledge that as individuals, we can challenge the meaning and impact that the Internet has on us—that's when we are in a position of power.

If social media is currently a toxic space for you, it is 100 percent possible to critique and analyze that experience. What content are you consuming and internalizing? Who are you letting impact your mind and energy—and in your offline spaces, too? We think that the experiences we have are not redefinable (I know that's not a word, but you get me), but they exist to be redefined, waiting for us to be just bold enough to do so. And the amazing thing about this is that when we disrupt the negative culture and create more positive online spaces, we let others in and *become* a safe space ourselves.

In what ways is social media currently toxic for you?

In what ways is social media currently positive for you?

....

....

....

....

....

....

THE CONTENT WE CONSUME

While I deeply care about social, environmental, and ethical justice, I cannot have devastating news and content at the forefront of my every day. This is not selfish, insensitive, or dismissive. This is nurturing the only energy I have. This is making sure that I am nourished and filled up with enough wonderful things so that I can better handle and contribute my energy to support others who are fighting to make profound change, and be a part of that journey as well. Some people may be able to handle constant news of hate and devastation and grieving, but it changes me. I don't feel as present; I don't feel like myself. When that content surrounds me on my timeline or on TV, I become more emotion than human—more angry, anxious, agitated.

Maybe you can relate to this feeling. Over time, the fear, judgment, hate, and anger become a part of us, just as much as the love, freedom of expression, care, and positivity can. So, to maintain my wellness, I check in here and there, vow to be a voice to help amplify when I can, and promise to do IRL work that brings awareness and tangible positive effects to people's lives. Because through the empowerment and transformation of an individual, we enable the same for whole communities.

I want you to do the same. *Unfollow* or minimize your interaction with the people and content that make you feel like you're losing brain cells, make you desire success rooted in material things or external success, make you want to hide from the world, and make you question your beauty, intelligence, and magic. Set boundaries with your well-being in mind. These people and spaces aren't going to mind you leaving, and if they do, that sounds like a them problem. Instead, seek the hidden gems of the Internet and real world that enliven your heart and spirit, make you want to be and do better, push you to question the thought patterns and beliefs you have, and most important, make you feel secure in yourself and appreciated. We can use the Internet to change our lives for the better, opening ourselves up to opportunities to grow and learn personally and professionally, make an impact, uplift others, start meaningful conversations, and feel a sense of belonging.

How many of your current fears and thoughts about yourself, other people, and places are based off social media influence?

....

....

....

....

Fears influenced by social media:

....

....

....

Thoughts influenced by social media:

Perceptions influenced by social media:

How can you improve your social media and Internet experience?

CREATING YOUR OWN ONLINE REALITY

Only within the past year have I fully embraced creating my own social media experience rather than adapting to the one that already exists.

I realized that my biggest fear was conflict and judgment. I didn't want to speak my mind about anything controversial because I didn't want to be hurt, lose followers, or be judged. Too many times I've had Internet bullies and trolls come for me under the most noncontroversial topics, like making vegan pizza or talking about my nonprofit work. They'd say things like "Health coach? More like fry girl at McDonald's" or "She looks thirty years old and sick" or "That's a horrible wig" (referring to my natural hair *insert eye roll*) or they'd call me literally every derogatory word in the dictionary. The list goes on and on. These comments made me want to close myself off and stay in my lane.

But I started to notice that being this smaller version of myself—more reserved, nonpolitical, and cookie cutter—made me unhappy and increasingly unfulfilled. I wanted to add dimension to the foundation I'd created and share my opinion on all the things I'm infatuated with and angry about and discovering while growing up. Letting strangers dictate how I contributed to my happiness and community increasingly seemed dumb. So, I slowly but surely started switching things up as I got more comfortable with sharing my truth, my whole self. Of course, this came with frustrating comments and conversations . . . but also a feeling in my gut that I was doing the right thing anyway. Not everyone has to or will ever understand me and what I'm going through and what I believe—and it's okay. *It's okay!* I don't have to be a people pleaser or "neutral" if I don't want to be.

And this applies to you, too. Just do what feels right when it feels right. Don't fear being authentic, not because it's a trend, but because authenticity is the fabric of who we are, waiting to be unraveled and allowed. Without trying, just being. So, speak up when you're ready, and close off when you need to. Often behind hate or anger is fear, so recognize that most criticisms or mean comments are just cries for attention or projections of fear that have nothing to do with you. Release these projections and tell your stories because they matter to you. All the rest you can't control . . . so why stress about it? Being your genuine self will intimidate some and attract many who appreciate the value you bring to the world.

Contrary to popular belief, the haters do not make me stronger. The lovers do. Negative energy can be transformed, but it's never as pure, electrifying, and transformative as the energy of genuine love and support. So, don't feel like you've got to keep the haters around. Be unafraid to use the block button or comment blocker to protect your energy and curate what is allowed within your space. The people who are supposed to resonate with and appreciate your presence and expression will do so. I've had the most incredible and life-changing realizations, conversations, and connections with people through social media because I'm finally using this platform in a way that is intentional, meaningful, and real.

HOW TO HEAL INTERNET BLUES

There are still days on the Internet that leave me exhausted and not feeling the best—whether it's an uncalled-for comment or exchange, a post that triggers insecurity, or overwhelming and upsetting content. That's why it's so important to not only create an on- and offline environment that keeps us in a good headspace, but also know how to nurture and refill our cups in more difficult times. If we don't, our emotions can easily whisk us into overanalyzing and internalizing our experiences online. So here are some things I've found helpful to do when the Internet has gotten to me and I need to step back and take care:

INVESTIGATE IT. ASK YOURSELF 5 QUESTIONS:

1. What triggered this and why?
2. Is this feeling true?
3. If it is true, why do I believe it?
4. What/who has made me believe this?
5. Why does it matter?

Usually by the time I mow through these questions in my head or on paper, I get to the conclusion that the feeling is false or just an unacknowledged, suppressed insecurity. Reaching this point allows me to reconstruct these beliefs and form a more positive opinion or dig deeper if need be.

COMPARING MYSELF OR MY LIFE

If you catch yourself envying or comparing yourself to someone, try thinking about and working through these things:

1. Make a list of the specific people and content that are triggering this emotion. Then write down how comparing yourself to these "online lives" might be wasting your time. Finally, write down what you feel you should do to minimize exposure to this trigger if it doesn't add any real value or meaning to your life. If you find that your comparison stems more from admiration than envy, write down the qualities you admire and what steps you can take to develop these characteristics. Do they inspire you to live better?

    Beyond this, take some time to consider if comparing yourself or criticizing others may be rooted in making you feel better about yourself. Sometimes we tear others down for a temporary self-esteem boost.

Acknowledge that this is destructive and blocks your blessings. When we support others in their wins and celebrate their successes it opens us up to success and support as well.

2.   Awareness has entered the chat. :) As you're on social media, actively participate in curating an experience that will be good for your mental well-being. If you can, in real time, honor your well-being by reevaluating the people you follow, hitting the block button, turning off comments, or taking a look at your habits—then you reinforce to yourself that your joy is the top priority and that you are in control of how you experience the Internet.

3.   Evaluate your values. Are the things you're comparing yourself or your life to based on something that truly represents your values, or the values projected onto you? Many of us grow up thinking that money and expensive things represent success, joy, and value . . . but as we've seen time and time again, money is just a tool and doesn't buy happiness. Happiness—along with success, value, and validity—are all in the eye of the beholder. For example, if you've always wanted to have expensive houses or expensive cars—are you buying happiness or validation? Do you just want to flex on others and feel superior? Always try and get to the root intention of these desires.

4.   Gratitude attitude. It's so simple that it can become difficult. We are constantly bombarded with reminders of what we don't have and what we "need"—but when we look at all we've got, like your pet who sees nothing but perfection when they gaze tenderly into your eyes—you can't help but feel your heart swell with gratefulness. Be grateful for how far you've made it, even with the slip-ups or bumpy roads. Be grateful for your heavy eyes that push you into sleep at night. When you can find just one thing to be grateful for, you help reduce feelings of unworthiness and comparison.

Meet Nia

NIA SIOUX is an eighteen-year-old actress, singer, and dancer who first became known for her role on the series *Dance Moms* before taking on a role in an off-Broadway show and becoming a series regular on the CBS daytime series *The Bold and the Beautiful*. Through her fan base of millions, she shares messages of positivity and empowerment, as well as the stories of people from all walks of life who are making a difference in the world.

I used to watch Nia on *Dance Moms* every now and then and see her strength and grace in dealing with an overwhelming amount of hate, criticism, and injustice from being on the show. Despite all of this, her kind heart and authenticity have always shone through. I was so surprised and grateful when she featured me on her Instagram #RoleModelMonday series a few years ago, and we have become friends since that surprise feature. Nia is an example of just how important it is to be kind and use our platforms for good. I deeply respect her dedication to making the world a little bit brighter in all the ways she expresses herself.

Haile: Take me through your journey and how you got to where you are today!

Nia: I started out on the TV show *Dance Moms* when I was around nine years old—just your normal kid from Pittsburgh who loved to dance. But throughout the show I was presented as the underdog. I was the only black girl, and I was getting body shamed—no one knew my full story or what I had gone through to get to that point. I was diagnosed with reflex neurovascular dystrophy and was unable to walk. Overcoming that was one of my greatest challenges. Growing up on camera was really hard; everyone saw me in my awkward phase . . . it was like living in a fishbowl in a way. But I was raised to stick it out and never quit, so I stayed to continue dancing with my friends, do what I love, and just work on not letting all the negativity get to me. And in the end, despite that negativity, it gave me a great platform to be where I am today. Since recently leaving the show, I'm now able to seriously pursue acting and music as well, which has been amazing. Before, no one really paid a lot of attention to me and thought I wouldn't do much outside of *Dance Moms*, so it feels good to prove everyone who didn't believe in me wrong and truly do what I love for a living.

Haile: **What was the turning point where you realized you had a responsibility to use your social media platform for positivity and sharing the goodness of others?**

Nia: I've grown up with a lot of positive influences in my life; I've always had love and support, and it is really a blessing to say that. It's because of my family that I've become comfortable with opening up on my personal experiences and helping others. And I just feel like the messages to spread positivity and stand up for myself have always been with me. But what really inspired me to start spreading positivity and sharing the work others are doing out in the world was my experience meeting so many people with amazing stories who didn't necessarily have the platform to share about them. I wanted to help people see different types of role models through all of the stories and lives out there. It's honestly an honor for me to share them!

Haile: **What does Living Lively mean to you?**

Nia: Living Lively means living your life to the fullest. Not being afraid of what's to come, to put yourself out there and do what you love. Expressing yourself the way that you want to, not how someone else wants you to. Learning from the past but not living in it—continuing to move forward.

You know, people take teens for granted. They're like "oh they don't know the meaning of life," but we've been through some stuff. The challenges we have faced with our limited life experience make us resilient and not afraid to face adversity.

FEELING DRAINED AND ANXIOUS

Step back and take a break. See how a couple days, a week, a month, without social media impact your energy levels and levels of anxiety. Is it FOMO, information overwhelm, or the pressure of unrealistic expectations that's at the root? Use this time to reflect and tap into your creativity and curiosity, which help to ground you.

When you step away and then return with awareness, it makes it easier to manage how social media impact you.

ACTION PLAN

"Social. No media." is something my dad says often—usually when my mom is taking photos of him to add to her Instastory (what can I say? Twenty-first-century parents, gotta love 'em). But this is true in a sense, in order to create and maintain wellness in the heart and mind, it is critically important to take the media away from the social and connect to the world and people beyond DMs, likes, and comments. So, what are five ways you can get to know your community, meet new people, and be more present and participatory IRL?

My 5 ways to be more social, with less media:

1. ....
....
....
....

2. ....
....
....
....

3. ....
....
....
....

4. ....
....
....

5. ....
....
....
....

POP 5
Education

For many of us, doing well in school is the first and most important responsibility we take on in our lives. With education systems being so heavily focused on perfection rather than trial, error, and discovery, we are trained to measure our worth and intelligence on being "perfect." It's a system that makes us view lack of understanding, mistakes, and slip-ups as indications that we are failures or not smart enough, even when none of this is true. When I was a kid, it felt like my whole identity was centered on school. As a matter of fact, since elementary school about 99.9 percent of my casual convos with adults always began with some kind of school-related comment or question, like, "Getting good grades, I hope!" "Staying in school? Making your parents proud?" and after high school, the classic "What's next?" and "Where are you headed?"

These interactions drill into our brains that our only focus as young people should be getting good grades in the subjects taught to us and moving up that ladder. But when we challenge what is normal, we're bound to be disruptive. And we're bound to create opportunity for us all to freely *dance and sing* to the beat of our own drums.

A NEW PERSPECTIVE ON EDUCATION

How different would your life be if those education-centered moments turned into conversations that prompted introspection? If the adults in your life asked you things like, "What makes you happy these days?" "What things would you like to learn?" "Are you making *yourself* proud?" "Following your own path or someone else's?" I think if we were asked these questions more often, even if we don't know the answers, it would prompt us to see that our value and intelligence don't just lie in report cards or degrees, that the construct of traditional education doesn't have to be stuck in one place, that our learning experiences can be unique to us, and that growth in other areas of our lives matters, too.

Of course, an education that equips you with the skills to function in society or do a specific job (such as medical school) is incredibly important. But our educational experiences can expand so far beyond what we could ever imagine. In a time with so much access to information, we no longer have to solely validate educational opportunities and experiences that are based on traditional models. The things you can learn from a knowledgeable influencer or elder in your community, from traveling, from an online course, from nature, from living and experiencing happiness and sadness, are all equally valid. This is all so powerful! Maybe you won't have a certificate to show for it, but life is all about how you learn and grow as an individual, whether others choose to acknowledge and validate that growth or not.

When I finally decided not to attend college last year, after contemplating it during middle and high school, I had to form a new perspective on education that could free me from feeling ashamed or "behind" because of my decision. I've had too many uncomfortable conversations with people who have criticized my choice to learn my way, warning that I'd fall behind and never be able to "catch up" to my peers. But we can't let someone else's limitations define our possibilities. I'll never catch up to my peers if I didn't even sign up for the race to begin with! No matter what anyone says, this life is ours to unravel and learn from. The mistakes and mishaps, risks and leaps of faith, "failures" and "successes" are all bound to happen no matter what path we choose.

What are some beliefs you hold about education?

....

....

....

....

Are the above beliefs entirely valid? What has influenced these beliefs?

....

....

What/who are the hidden teachers in your life?

....

....

....

....

CUSTOMIZED LEARNING

By the end of middle school I was ridiculously stressed out and overwhelmed by the idea of high school and the work I was doing traveling and speaking across the country. I had already experienced the stress of missing more than one hundred days of school, catching up on tests, and feeling like I was wasting way too much time learning about every. single. type. of. cloud and things I will never use, like the Pythagorean Theorem (much respect to my guy Pythagoras, though). Knowing that I could've used all that brain power, time, and energy to build my nonprofit or learn about things that I cared about bothered me on the daily. Moving forward, I knew I wanted my educational experience to be purposeful and very intentional. For me, that looked like business courses on nonprofit management and sustainability and digging deeper into wellness and nutrition education. There was a moment when I had to either choose to follow the traditional educational path or commit to the uncharted path. And after some serious convincing and several PowerPoints for my extremely detail- and outcome-oriented dad, my parents allowed me to try online courses for high school. I never could have dreamed just how much that freedom and flexibility would open up my educational opportunities. Through customized learning, I was able to focus on projects that brought me joy, strengthen my speaking and teaching skills through experience, graduate high school early, and graduate as the youngest Integrative Nutrition Health Coach in the United States from the Institute for Integrative Nutrition in 2016. All thanks to taking a chance on customized education!

As one of the most valuable privileges we have in the twenty-first century, customizing our educational experiences gives us immense power. Almost anything we want to learn about is accessible—YouTube videos, Google research sessions, online certification courses, multigenerational/multicultural discussions, and so much more. With this accessibility comes an unbelievable opportunity to make our educational experience fit our lives rather than the other way around. We can center our learning on topics that actually interest us, follow programs that fit our lifestyles, and fast-track the development of certain skills.

Luckily, you don't have to be homeschooled or getting a nontraditional education to tap into this opportunity. No matter who you are and where you're from, as long as you own a smartphone or have access to a computer, the opportunity to shift your mind-set and learn about *anything* is always there. You can start a business, follow an interest, create community—the choice is yours.

List 3 things you want to learn, and how this would contribute to your life:

1. ....

....

....

2. ....

....

....

3. ....

....

....

TAPPING INTO CURIOSITY

Curiosity is a lost art. How often are we encouraged to challenge the ideas and structures in place? How often are we required or expected to seek true understanding? In elementary school, I was *that* kid who never stopped interrupting lessons to ask questions. I had some good teachers who, thankfully, fostered that curiosity, but sadly in the fourth grade I had a teacher who shut that curiosity down and made me feel ashamed and dumb for asking questions. I didn't want to face the embarrassment of hearing I'd asked enough questions or that she'd explained the topic "enough," so I shut down my curiosity in school for quite some time.

We've been conditioned and trained to take information at face value and to avoid questioning in fear of conflict or being perceived as annoying. But digging deeper helps conversations and learning moments truly expand! It's where a powerful shift in how educators and students interact with each other begins, helping to build safer spaces where we can respectfully agree and disagree as we debate.

The thing is, curiosity requires vulnerability and courage. It requires us to prioritize our curiosity over the opinions of others. To admit that we don't know enough and want to learn more, and to be okay with any unknown reaction or ripple effects—good or bad. Through tapping into curiosity, you can learn so much about the world, yourself, and others.

In what ways can you open yourself up to more vulnerable curiosity?

....

....

....

....

I THINK WE'RE *ALL* TEACHERS AND STUDENTS

There is so much wisdom beyond the traditional halls of education. This wisdom is present in all types of people, not just people who have the benefit of advanced age. Of course, opportunities to acquire wisdom happen over time, but wisdom does not automatically come with age. What matters is paying attention to what happens in our lives and adjusting our mind-set, actions, and intentions accordingly. My generation is getting wiser younger because we can easily connect with and learn from both the shared and the unique realities of others—recognizing the thread of commonality connecting each of our lives.

At the end of the day, when all the labels are removed, we're the same. We may not share the same race, gender, sexual orientation, income, or age—but there is always something humans can connect on, share, or teach: A love of food, family, art. Hard times and challenges. Victories and transformations. Humanity.

When we understand that our stories and experiences are valuable, we can become simultaneously mentor and mentee to ourselves and others. Be open to learning from anyone—and teaching anyone!

Name an experience that taught you something invaluable:

....

....

....

....

....

....

Name something you believe you can (and/or want to) teach others:

....

....

....

....

....

....

....

....

Meet Gabrielle

GABRIELLE JORDAN is twenty years old, an international speaker, and the owner of Jewelz of Jordan, a luxury jewelry business, which she started at the age of nine. She is also the cofounder of the ExCEL Youth Mentoring Institute, a youth-based online mentoring organization providing mentorship opportunities and educational resources for entrepreneurship and leadership development. Gabrielle has personally engaged and inspired over fifteen thousand people of all ages across the globe and has been featured on TLC, the *Harry* show, and in the Huffington Post, and has worked with Columbia University, Google, and United Way, to name a few.

When I was just getting started with my activism journey at age ten, I heard about

Gabrielle's work and felt so comforted knowing that there was another black girl out in the world making a difference and disrupting the norm. After following each other on social media for years, we finally connected when Gabby interviewed me for her podcast. And the rest is history! Her dedication and tenacity are contagious, and it's humbling to see her move about the world with such intention and tangible impact.

Haile: **How did your entrepreneurial and mentorship journey start? What gave you the confidence to step into a leader/mentor/educator role at such a young age?**

Gabrielle: When I was nine years old, I started my jewelry business making high-quality pieces for women using natural stones and freshwater pearls. Making jewelry was something that I always loved to do. I started learning when I was seven and then went to school and started selling my creations, and it kind of progressed into a business by the time I was nine. I wanted to start a business because I loved making jewelry and it was a good way to make money, but I started to realize that my age was a factor, and adults would be very surprised about how old I was to be doing what I was doing. And kids would be surprised and ask me how I got started and how they could do it, too.

I didn't really expect this, but I saw I had an opportunity to inspire but also educate other young people on what's possible for them, and how waiting until you're an adult to start a career or go after a goal was a societal limitation they didn't have to stick to. So I wrote a book when I was eleven years old called *The Making of a Young Entrepreneur: A Kid's Guide to Developing the Mind-Set for Success*. The idea was to teach kids not just the steps to starting a business, but also the mind-set behind being a young entrepreneur. And from there I became a speaker and cofounded the ExCEL Youth Mentoring Institute with my mom, because we really wanted to be able to mentor, support, and provide the tools and education to young people starting businesses. We wanted to become the village that some kids don't have.

Haile: What's your advice for someone who wants to mentor others or teach them a skill but doesn't believe they're experienced enough?

Gabrielle: I don't think you have to be an expert in order to teach, and I think the best teachers are willing to learn from their students and make it a mutual learning experience. If schools were set up in a way where students and teachers had actual discussions versus the traditional "information deposit" method, we would learn so much more. Also, we should always keep ourselves informed, be cautious about the validity of what we share, and yet be willing to help if we feel we have something of value to contribute.

Haile: What does Living Lively mean to you?

Gabrielle: When I think of Living Lively, I think about finding joy in all the pieces of your life. I think happiness is incredibly important, but joy is something that lasts. It's a continuing thing. When we find joy in our lives—including even the hard times, because we recognize the potential for something good to come from it—that's when we're Living Lively.

It's also about being confident, because for a long time I had this nervousness about discussing and talking about myself outside of business settings, like with friends. I was so nervous at the idea that I'd lose friends because I seemed too intimidating or too successful, so I would hide this part of me away. But recently I've experienced a lot of things that have changed my perspective on what confidence means. The moment I decided to stop living in that fear of being too much for people was the moment that I started realizing who I really am and gaining true confidence and boldness. This started a ripple effect and changed the way I do everything. I can finally feel happy about myself.

Also, I think most of us come to this point in our lives when we realize we either don't know who we are, we've lost sight of who we are, or we never really knew who we were. It's this moment of recognition and asking yourself—who am I? And when you can finally investigate and answer that question is when you can genuinely Live Lively and find joy in an authentic life that is truly yours. You're no longer living in a template. There's something very powerful in knowing you're following your own path.

ACTION PLAN

There is great power in acknowledging that, yes, the world may be set up a certain way, but we create our realities and we can choose to operate off of our own definitions and standards—not anyone else's. Deconstructing and reshaping societal and systemic constructs, norms, and ideas is essential for progress. Write down how you can expand your definition of education, being educated, and learning.

How is (or has) traditional education propelled you forward?

....

....

....

....

....

How is traditional education holding you back?

....

....

....

....

....

How would you like to redefine or evolve your educational experience?

....

....

....

....

....

What can you learn from your life outside of school?

....

....

....

....

....

How can you engage in curiosity?

....

....

....

....

....

POP 6
World Perspective

It's a really *strange* time to be alive, right? We simultaneously see incredible technological advances, unlimited personal freedom, unnecessary human suffering, and unacceptable disrespect toward certain people based on what they look like, what they believe, who they love, and where they come from. We have more access and connectivity than ever before but can't seem to fully use them to heal and progress. This is because of stereotypes, biases, pride, money, and monster egos. How individuals see the world creates the world. And this is part of why we are constantly in the midst of opportunity and oppression, division and unity.

Sometimes it seems like the world is split in half, with polar opposite points of view constantly going head-to-head. But at the core of almost every human is the need to be loved, validated, significant, and safe. We aren't really strangers or enemies; we're just a bunch of people trying to find a place in this world. And sometimes that place can be rooted in hate, fear, or insecurity disguised by inferiority complexes.

We've heard time and time again the phrase "hurt people hurt people," and it couldn't be truer. I think a whole lot of us are really hurt right now. We're feeling trapped in our circumstances, by shifting traditions, toxic relationships, financial struggles, lack of access to resources, and by ignoring and undernourishing the things that bring us joy. We internalize the vices of humanity. These feelings have to go somewhere, and if we're not taught how to cope in healthy ways, we latch on to anything that can help us feel better or more purposeful. Some people will do anything to belong, or to hold on to what's comfortable.

HOW WE SEE THE WORLD

The way we see the world is a foundational element of who we are and how we feel. As you know, we spend years soaking in the mind-sets, biases, and views of the people we're most consistently exposed to, and when we can't connect to the stories of people outside this group, it creates space for us to latch on to false narratives and perceptions. This also applies to how we view our potential. If we grow up surrounded by disempowered individuals, that disempowered mind-set infects us as well and will continue to plague our thoughts, actions, and attitude toward life if not interrupted by a new and more positive influence. All the isms and phobias that exist come from people who have recycled and passed on false beliefs that they have left unchallenged.

The power of rethinking our personal and world views can bring us closer to figuring out not only who we really are, but also who we can really show up as in our communities and beyond. And remember, inner work creates the outer world. So, as we continue to search for more joy, kindness, and love within, it will be reflected in our external experiences as well.

List 3 major societal biases or perceptions you currently hold that are not evidence/fact-based:

1. ....

....

....

2. ....

....

....

3. ....

....

....

Why do you hold these beliefs?

....

....

....

....

....

....

....

....

List 3 major perceptions of your potential you currently hold that are not evidence/fact-based:

1. ....

....

....

2. ....

....

....

3. ....

....

....

Why do you hold these beliefs?

....

....

....

....

....

....

....

....

RESHAPING OUR PERSPECTIVES

Confronting our beliefs takes a lot of effort and true interest in showing up as better versions of ourselves. It is so much easier to have anger, fear, loneliness, and confusion fuel our motivations and actions than to question who we are, what we believe, and how much of it is really *us*. Some of us, seriously, hate just to hate. And yes, it's simple to write off these people as "haters" or "trolls," but, at the end of the day, they are just reflections of their environment, and their behavior is a cry for help, love, and attention. It is daring to have compassion for people like this, and ourselves, to begin to reshape our perspectives.

Here are some moves you can make to get started:

STEP OUTSIDE YOUR SOCIAL AND ENVIRONMENTAL BUBBLE. On- or offline! Volunteer in a community you don't know much about. Follow people on social media that lead a different life than you. Read books written by diverse authors to take in new perspectives (this just might be that book).

DIVERSIFY WHO YOU TALK TO . . . AND RESPECT THEM. You don't have to agree. With cancel culture, we are increasingly alienating individuals who may not share the same values or opinions as we do. This is toxic. No one is required to agree with anyone, but seeking to understand instead of just judging can lead us to so much deeper, fuller conversations and truths that could open the door to real solutions. Be open to conversations that offer opportunities for critiquing, educating, and learning, taking a seat and standing up. Show kindness. Set boundaries, prioritize respect, speak your truth, and determine who and what is worth your energy. Strive to create connections and community that you and others can be challenged by and learn from, but also feel safe in.

LISTEN MORE DEEPLY. Today we have a lot of echo chambers with people just waiting to hear their own voices. It is becoming rare that we are fully present when talking to others. Whether it's because of distractions like our phones or our own minds thinking about how we'll respond, we aren't hearing each other. When someone chooses to open up or engage with us, we should respect and acknowledge that act.

Meet Hannah

HANNAH TESTA is a seventeen-year-old sustainability advocate, international speaker, and founder of Hannah4Change, an organization dedicated to fighting issues that impact the planet. She shares her passion for people, the planet, and animals by partnering with businesses and government to influence them to develop more sustainable practices. Hannah has received numerous honors and awards, including Teen Earth Day Hero by CNN, the Young Superhero for Earth Award by Captain Planet, and the Gloria Barron Prize.

I first met Hannah and learned about the incredible work she does through a partnership with Kashi. Becoming friends and following her journey over the past four years or so has truly been an honor. I've seen firsthand her passion and dedication to being a prominent voice in our world, spreading kindness, and making a difference.

Haile: **How do you see the world?**

Hannah: The world is filled with some troubling issues, including animal cruelty, pastic pollution, the climate crisis, and endangered animal species, as well as some of the most daunting environmental challenges of our time. We all need to speak up and take action to make the world a better place, because if we don't, who will? The biggest challenge we face is the expectation that someone else will save us. I try to live my life by speaking up for the voiceless and making my voice heard, whether it is to business leaders, politicians, or everyday citizens. And despite the challenges in the world, and all of the negativity, I do my best to keep a positive attitude and make at least one impactful change each day.

Haile: How and when did you start learning about environmental issues? What made you believe that even with such huge issues to tackle, you could make a difference?

Hannah: I started to learn about the world's environmental issues when I was around the age of ten. I started to become aware of all these issues happening all across the globe, and I knew I couldn't sit back and watch it all happen. I first started by volunteering, getting involved as much as I could with other organizations and taking part in their campaigns. Then I started to do my own fundraisers, campaigns, and speaking. Ever since, I've been continuing this work all across the world.

I realized that many people, including myself at one point, are ignorant of many of the issues affecting our world (not necessarily by choice, but just don't know what's happening). Once I became aware of these issues, I knew I had to do something, and I felt that if other people became educated on these issues, they, too, would take action or change their daily habits that make an impact. So many big issues in the world can seem overwhelming, and trust me they are, but no one can single-handedly save the world. It's a team effort, it takes a village, and I'm using my voice to join with the millions of other people to stop these issues before it is too late.

Haile: What does Living Lively mean to you?

Hannah: To me, Living Lively means living beyond the stereotypes and the status quo and living life to the fullest. Our time on this earth is very limited, and tomorrow is never guaranteed, but Living Lively is using the time you have to do things you are afraid to do, working toward your dreams, and spending quality time with friends and family. It also requires you to take care of yourself by being mindful of the nutrients (or junk) you are putting into your body. Burnout is definitely real, and I have experienced feeling overworked, so self-care is very important. And I try to cherish what I'm doing. Whether it's walking the dog, meeting someone new, or playing with my brother, I try to keep a positive attitude, because your attitude can alter your whole day. Despite your situation, your struggles, and your environment, if you have a positive attitude you can survive and thrive, and that positive attitude will have an impact that will last long after you're gone.

IDENTIFY ROOT CAUSES. The actions above are all great steps. But if we don't look into the core of our perceptions, they're useless. What fuels your perceptions? Is it attention? Loneliness? Feeling lost or needing direction? Anger? Fear? Hold this space with grace and love for yourself and the process. We all have the ability to transform into new versions of ourselves every day. Let go of who you believe you have to be and start to question what already lies beyond the surface.

ACTION PLAN

It's sometimes scary when we realize our lives are in our own hands. I think that's one of the hardest-hitting feelings of growing up. Suddenly, every move has a consequence. And yes, there are circumstances we can't control—but how we react and move forward is entirely up to us. This is where all the freedom to be and become whoever we want lies. And dismantling the lies we've been told and have repeated to ourselves is one of the first steps. Take some time to look at your world and who you are within it:

How can you start to dismantle the beliefs and perceptions that impact your worldview?

What do you want to contribute to the lives of others?

....

....

....

....

....

....

How can you change the way you see and interact with the world?

....

....

....

....

....

....

Creativity and Community

Creativity is a collection of inspirations, experiences, and dreams expressed as our external DNA. It is permission to do what we love. It is an invitation to adventure. But most important, creativity is an entry point. It's a door to innovation that can change lives and create deep connections with ourselves and with people we will never meet. For me, cooking and writing are two of my outlets for expression and connection. It's incredible that I am able to connect with each of you through articulation of my life experiences and the recipes in this book that I created in my home kitchen—inspired by special moments in my life.

In our society, though, the value of creativity is typically measured by profitability rather than the impact on the heart or mind. We're told horror stories about "starving artists," and how doing what we love is almost always associated with being broke. This perception is what contributes to losing our innate creativity as we get older and start to believe we have to do something of "value"—something more left-brained and logic-based. But, now more than ever, we need people who can shake things up by coloring outside the lines. We need art of all kinds that can speak to us, inspire us, and move us to take action. And at the end of the day, computers will never be able to compete with the innovation of the creative mind. The ability to imagine the unimagined, discover intersections, cultivate curiosity, and bring things to life is truly magic in action! When we can get into the groove of expressing ourselves authentically and connecting our creativity, talents, and passions to a bigger purpose, we start to drop perfectionism and unlock true joy in creating, just because we can and we're alive! There is no longer a need to fit our expression inside a box.

HOW CREATIVITY TRANSFORMS

Getting lost in creativity forces us to jump into the moment and out of our heads. Creative focus frees us from mental traps of perfection and judgment, because we never really know what our creations may be until they're done. That spontaneity and freedom allows us to open up, rejuvenate, and grow. And it gives us the opportunity to cultivate curiosity and challenge the world around us. Another great thing about the impact of creativity is that it can help us find our voice and a type of fulfillment that isn't dependent on others. We become more self-sufficient and start to improve the relationships we have and how we communicate with and see the world.

How is creativity freeing to you?

....

....

How can you cultivate more creativity?

....

....

....

WHAT DRIVES US TO CREATE

A big piece of Living Lively is striving to live with intention and inner freedom. Finding the why behind what we create gives us an understanding of how it serves us and can serve others. Do we write poetry or songs to work through emotions? Do we take photos of nature to express gratitude or of people to capture and tell stories? Do we doodle to free our minds and let go? Often within creative activities that matter to and impact us lies an opportunity to connect to the heart of community through that very thing.

What are some different ways you are (or can be) creative? You can list both traditional and nontraditional ways!

....

....

....

What are some causes or issues in the world you're passionate about that could be supported by your creative outlet or talent?

....

....

....

What are some ways you could connect your creativity to community?

....

....

Meet Maya

I was introduced to Maya and her work through a viral TED talk she gave a few years back on intentional entrepreneurship, creativity, and sustainability. Through her video, I instantly connected to her beautiful spirit, authenticity, and determination to be a force of change in this world. And just a couple years later we found ourselves both being honored as M.A.D. Girls at the 2016 BET Black Girls Rock awards show. We quickly became friends, and it has been such a joy supporting and watching each other as we've grown personally and professionally.

Haile: Have you always been a creative? Where did your journey start? And did you realize you wanted to connect your creative talents with a bigger purpose and environmental activism?

Maya: I've been a creative for as long as I can remember! I've been drawing basically since I could hold a crayon, I started making animated flip books when I was four, and I started my eco-fashion design brand when I was eight. Art has always been a big part of my life and who I am as a person.

It's always been instilled in me to try to make a positive difference in my community and in the world. I knew that giving back to the

MAYA PENN is the award-winning twenty-year-old founder and CEO of the sustainable fashion brand Maya's Ideas, eco-designer, three-time TED speaker, global activist, social entrepreneur, filmmaker, philanthropist, and author. She was selected by Oprah Winfrey as her youngest SuperSoul 100 entrepreneur, change maker, and thought leader. She also does consulting for major fashion brands on how to shift into and incorporate eco-friendly fashion and sustainable company practices. Maya knows firsthand just how powerful and transformative creativity and giving back can be.

earth was something that I wanted to make a priority no matter what I did in life, so it was only natural that I used my passion for art to drive my activism.

Haile: **Advice for anyone who is afraid to unleash their creativity or use their voice or advocate for what they believe in? And any first steps anyone can take to connect their creativity, talents, and passions to global issues?**

Maya: If not now, when? The world is in need of creatives, innovators, change makers, and thought leaders. The smallest actions can lead to the biggest changes; it's up to everyone to take action.

Many people think they don't have enough influence, knowledge, experience, money, or power to make a change. It's easy for people to feel like a drop in the bucket. But the truth is, every drop creates a ripple effect. Identify the passions and the issues you zero in on. Is there some way you can use your skills, interests, and so on to make a difference? Whether it's using art to advocate, starting an initiative to make an impact, or raising money to give back, be creative on how you can start something awesome to make a difference. Also, look for areas of need. Can you start an initiative in your school or community? Are there organizations or nonprofits that you would like to be a part of? Reach out. There's so much opportunity to make change.

Haile: **What does Living Lively mean to you?**

Maya: I think Living Lively is living your truth, doing what makes your soul happy, and doing something to give back. To never underestimate the power of believing in yourself and what you care about. To use what you're passionate about to make a positive impact on the world.

ACTION PLAN

Creativity is a force to be reckoned with! It is the core of finding answers to the world's biggest issues, creating more jobs, and helping us all feel a little happier and thrive a little more. Creativity makes us powerful in our own way and it must be nurtured and supported as much as we can to spread love and new perspectives. Dig into some ways you can strengthen your relationship with creativity!

What are some things holding you back from being creative?

....

....

....

....

How can you nourish your creativity daily?

....

....

....

....

Set your top 5 creative goals:

My 5 creative goals are:

1. ....

....

....

2. ....

....

....

3. ....

....

....

4. ....

....

....

5. ....

....

....

Live Lively

PUTTING IT ALL INTO ACTION

I hope that these 7 Points of Power and the stories of these incredible individuals made you feel something good—whether it's feeling more at peace with your journey in POP 2 or beginning to rethink the systems and beliefs you hold yourself by in POP 5 and 6, just know you're on the right track! And remember, there is no pressure to be perfect as you explore and put these seven points into action. Interpret and act on them in whatever way speaks to you—even just increasing awareness of your inner power is something to be really proud of! Commit to being an active creator of your present and future and to always treating yourself with the utmost respect and kindness. It's not always easy, but when you've got your own back and best interest at heart, truly nothing can stop you from living your liveliest life!

Before jumping into allll the tips on fueling your body with recipes that bring health, adventures in the kitchen, and joy, I want to leave you with a little wisdom from my little sis, Nia!

Her wisdom is an example of something I touched on in POP 5. There is no age cap on the impact and wisdom someone can impart to us. My little sister, I, and so many of you reading this are growing up in a time when living for ourselves and in the moment isn't always popular. But I truly believe it's the key to helping us feel true happiness when we wake up every day—knowing we are loved, valuable, and worth all the self-respect in the world.

Nia's Nugget of Wisdom

Living Lively is living full and true, not doing what we do for anybody else, but really living for ourselves, because these days so many people are living for social media and to show off their "best" life moments. For me Living Lively is ultimately a bunch of moments that just make me feel complete. It's hard to explain, but it's personal. For me, it's when I'm creating art or spending time with my dog, Roxy. Try to remind yourself that no matter what yesterday was, today is a new day. Don't be too hard on yourself, and keep yourself in check to be grateful. Try to live in the moment and connect with the people in your life.

PART II

Recipes

Let's Get Cookin', Good Lookin'!
(BEFORE YOU GET STARTED)

Food is one of the three keys to my heart. (Yes, I have *three* keys to my heart. . . . And what about it?!) Food is where some of my favorite, most nostalgic memories stem from; it's where the life and career I lead today began; it's through food that I find joy, adventure, and nourishment. Developing a healthy relationship with food and cooking is invaluable, because it has the power to, quite literally, give us life and fill us up both physically and emotionally. It connects us through culture and flavor and humbles us through trial and error. Plus! There's simply nothing like the level of pride that comes from feasting on a home-cooked meal filled with love that is brilliantly delicious *and* fuels your precious body to keep pushing on.

Before we dive in, I want you to truly open your arms to this journey in the kitchen, no matter what level you're at:

WHAT'S YOUR CURRENT COOKING SKILL LEVEL?
HOW FAR DO YOU WANT TO GO?

* **SCARED BUT WILLING**

  (Fears grocery stores, knives, and stoves—but willing to learn!)

* **WATER BURNER**

  (Can't seem to figure out water, but keeps pushing on)

* **ONE-DISH PONY**

  (Masters one dish, repeats dish for eternity)

* **KINDA COOKER**

  (Can utilize basic kitchen equipment to make staple foods)

* **BOILER AND STEAMER**

  (Thinks veggies can only be served with the life cooked out of them)

* **RECIPE RELIGIOUS**

  (Cooks only from recipes; a little intimidated by wandering too far)

* **FREQUENT FREESTYLER**

  (Knows how to whip up a lil something something out of nothing)

* **ALMOST A TOTAL BOSS**

  (Can confidently bring food to a potluck; probably into unusual ingredients)

* **ABSOLUTE PRO**

  (Creates flavor profiles, into nice plating and fusion creations—probably has a food account on Instagram)

* **CULINARY WIZARD**

  (Maybe has an award-winning food blog or cooking show—wait. Why are you reading this book??)

Wherever you're starting, be open to *allll* the fails and victories bound to be made. You might mess up once or twice (shout-out to the worst cupcakes I've ever made—sesame seed oil cupcakes!). You'll probably severely burn something, or make a tragically horrific mess of your kitchen! (Which I do Every.

Single. Time. I. Cook. BTW.) You'll also enjoy many memorable meals, grubbed on over great conversation! You'll experience the thrill of trying new spices and ingredients! And you'll love the way your body loves you back when you show it some much needed TLC. All in all, cooking can be fun, frustrating, and freeing—sometimes all at once. Embrace the adventure!

WHY PLANT-POWERED?

No matter how many times you might've rolled your eyes and secretly thought of a plan to get rid of the veggies on your plate (without eating them) as a little kid, there's no denying plants are reeeally good for us. I mean, there's got to be a reason why almost every mother on this planet told us to eat our fruits and vegetables, right?

Plants are magic, and scientists agree. Research shows that the more real and whole plant foods we eat, like fruits, veggies, legumes, and nutritious grains, we decrease the risk of developing conditions like heart disease, type 2 diabetes,

and obesity—and have better digestion, higher energy levels, and clearer minds. And the cool thing about plants is that even if we don't eat them exclusively, they still work to protect our bodies and help neutralize the toxins we consume. Mind-blowing, right?

Luckily, you don't have to be vegan, vegetarian, pescatarian, or follow any specific diet/lifestyle to enjoy plants and the recipes in this book . . . you simply have to be open. Eating more plants or being fully plant-powered is not about perfection or deprivation. It's about exploring real, whole foods, getting nourished, creating a better relationship and connection with our bodies, and paying attention to what we eat and how it makes us feel mentally, emotionally, and physically. Wellness is not one-size-fits-all, so let go of the traditional ideas of what "healthy" is and discover what that looks like for you. No matter how big or small the steps you take toward wellness are, they're still steps—and that's all that matters!

When you're aware and intentional about what you put into your body, your food preferences will start to change in favor of fueling your best self. And then the not-so-healthy cravings start to fade away, you stop counting calories and start tracking quality, and your body begins to thank you for filling it up with all the good stuff.

And BTW, despite stereotypes, eating more plants and engaging in wellness isn't just for white people or those who may be financially privileged. See Eating Lively on a Budget! (page 117) and my tips on how to make more affordable recipe and ingredient adjustments (page 122)!

RAPID-FIRE FAQ
WHAT NUTRITION DO I GET FROM PLANTS?

A balanced vegan diet is a nutrition powerhouse. Whole-plant foods—fruits and veggies, nuts, peas, beans, legumes, and grains—are bursting with life and contain nearly all the essential nutrients we need. All of the calcium, protein, fiber, iron, omega-3s, antioxidants, vitamins, minerals, and more are readily available in plant foods—therefore reducing LDL "bad" cholesterol (too much LDL can contribute to blocked arteries and higher risk of heart disease), providing heart-healthy benefits, boosting energy, and improving digestion! Look out for vitamin B12!—because B12 is rarely present in plants due to degraded soil quality, you'll need to take a supplement for this! Vitamin D is another one to look out for as it isn't present in many plant foods—try eating mushrooms like maiitake and portobello more often, consuming vitamin D fortified plant milks and grain products, spending 5 to 30 minutes in the sunshine each day, or supplementing with some drops to get this vitamin in!

WHERE CAN I GET MY PROTEIN?

This is probably the number one question asked of a vegan diet. But, for the millionth time, I am happy to break the confusion and announce that, *yes, plants contain protein. A lot of it, too! I meeaaan, cows are vegan. Do we ever wonder where they get the protein that gives us protein? Anyhooo,* let's get to the facts. Yes, plants have protein, and you can get an incredible amount of protein from foods like:

* EDAMAME: about 17 grams protein per cup
* TOFU: about 10 grams protein per ½ cup
* TEMPEH: about 31 grams protein per cup
* BEANS AND LEGUMES (HIGHEST IN PROTEIN): lentils, split peas, pinto beans, chickpeas, black beans, and navy beans
* NUTS AND SEEDS (HIGHEST IN PROTEIN): hemp seeds, pumpkin seeds, peanuts, almonds
* GRAINS (HIGHEST IN PROTEIN): teff, quinoa, wild rice, millet
* VEGGIES (HIGHEST IN PROTEIN): green peas, spinach, asparagus, Brussels sprouts

Now, remember, our protein needs are just as unique as we are and depend on our age, gender, and state of health. So you may need more or less depending on those factors!

Soy is a plant protein packed with fiber, calcium, iron, and other vitamins/minerals. Typical soy foods are tofu, tempeh, edamame, miso, and soy milk.

With all these fantastic benefits, how did we get so confused about (and scared of) soy? Well, it all started with a big misunderstanding. You see, high levels of the hormone estrogen have been linked to an increased risk for heart attacks, stroke, and breast cancer. But the confusion here comes from the fact that soy contains isoflavones, which are plant estrogens, and their chemical structure is very similar to human estrogen. However, plant estrogens bind to the body's estrogen receptors differently and function differently from human ones. In isolated cell studies, plant estrogens have been shown to activate genes that slow down and destroy the growth of cancer cells by supporting the body's antioxidant defenses and DNA repair.

But be smart with your soy! Add soy to your diet through non-GMO, traditional forms like tempeh, tofu, soy milks, and edamame. Limit overprocessed foods like soy nuggets or meats.

EARTH LOVE (ENVIRONMENTAL BENEFITS)

What I love about being vegan/plant-powered is that what I put on my fork impacts so much more than my body—it becomes a politicized act of solidarity and support of our planet. For each meal we choose to be plant-powered, we're also choosing to help our planet heal from generations and generations of damage and decrease our chances of our own extinction and the further extinction of other earth inhabitants.

RAPID-FIRE FACTS

* Animal agriculture produces more greenhouse-gas emissions than all forms of transportation *combined,* while eating more plants is associated with the greatest reductions in these emissions.

* Nearly two-thirds of all soybeans, corn, and barley and one-third of all grains are used as feed for the animals we overproduce. This food supply could easily alleviate hunger around the world if we collectively reduce our intake of animal products.
* By 2048, we could see completely fishless oceans due to the increasing depletion of the world's fisheries.
* As much as 91 percent of the Amazon rain forest destruction is due to animal agriculture.

If you care about climate change, increase the amount of plants on your plate!

FAM NOT FOOD (ETHICAL WINS)

My first introduction to animal cruelty was in 2014 when I watched the documentary *Earthlings* for the first time. I had just gone vegan and, as one does, I fell down a rabbit hole of layers and layers of what this compassionate lifestyle was really all about. Watching this documentary was tough and emotionally taxing. Discovering the way animals are treated in the agriculture, fashion, and entertainment industries left me feeling sick and overwhelmed. It truly changed my life and my perspective on the value of the beings that live not below us, but alongside us on this planet.

Six years ago you would literally *never* have seen me holding or loving on a cat, let alone a cow or pig. I had a severe phobia of most animals (except for very small dogs) and couldn't interact with them without being creeped out or scared. It didn't register with me that they were capable of feeling joy or pain and expressing themselves in similar ways to me. In my mind, beyond pets, animals were just food. I had "nothing in common" with them. They existed solely for consumption. But it is incredible to think that my journey through veganism has brought me to a point where I can recognize and appreciate the commonality between myself, our human race, and all the beings we share this planet with. And this awareness of both their suffering and happy moments allowed me to finally deconstruct the block I had against connecting to animals on a physical level. Through this experience, I've seen just how transformative compassion, acknowledgment, and understanding truly is. Eating plants has given me not just health, but more love in my heart.

RAPID-FIRE FACTS

* Approximately 9 percent—more than 850 million—of the animals raised for food in the United States each year never make it to the slaughterhouse because they have already died from stress-induced disease or injury.

* Four or more egg-laying hens are packed into a battery cage, a wire enclosure so small that none can spread her wings. Being held in such close confines, the hens peck at each other's feathers and bodies.

* Approximately 260 million male chicks are killed upon hatching in the United States each year because they won't lay eggs or be used for meat and therefore have no economic value.

* Calves can be taken away from their mothers mere moments after birth, causing distress for both. Calves raised for veal are so severely confined they cannot turn around or stretch their limbs.

GOING PLANT-POWERED WHEN YOUR FAMILY IS NOT

Learning about and profoundly connecting with something that feels really important can be such an exciting time. But the ability to try new things and further embark on a path of self-discovery isn't always easy, especially when the people around us don't understand or support the changes we want to make—let alone want to join us. So how can you embark on a journey of compassion, health, and sustainability when your family isn't (yet) on board?

It can be challenging dealing with naysayers, but there are subtle ways to show your strength, stand up for your choices, and get support. I hope these tips can help you feel more motivated, less alone, and ease any frustration. Here are the best things to do:

1. LEAD WITH COMPASSION

In the earlier 7 Points of Power, we discussed that our immediate thoughts and actions are often influenced by people in our lives, our upbringings, and media. When it comes to a plant-powered diet, there's been a particular (false) narrative surrounding the diet for decades that is just now being dismantled. We've grown up being told that animal products were a substantial and mandatory source of nutrition, but we're now learning that this is far from the truth. We can't avoid the science that proves the things we're used to eating are detrimental to the well-being of people, animals, and the planet.

Disruption of what is comfortable is bound to bring discomfort and skepticism; this is only human. A lack of exposure to facts along with firm, unquestioned beliefs create a sort of complex that is tied up in ego, genuine concern, or just stubbornness rooted in fear of something new. It's often about them and never entirely about us. Maybe they have failed at making similar lifestyle changes in the past and are projecting their outcome onto your potential. When you view adverse reactions from this perspective, it lessens the impact of it. Approach people who act from this place in a compassionate and relatable manner; don't set them up for resistance. We've all been in a position of unawareness and illusion, and that is okay. Let others take the time they need; the more humble and kind we are with the ways we share the things we're learning and putting into action, the more we let people feel safe in asking questions and supporting our journeys.

2. EDUCATION

To effectively educate others, we have to be somewhat aware of our intentions in doing so. Get to know your own reasons behind wanting to embark on a plant-powered journey. Is it compassion and love for sentient beings? Protecting our planet? Getting healthier? All three? Deeply understand and educate

yourself on why you're committing to giving this a go is super important! It helps you better explain that your choices are not a "phase," but informed and rooted in real intention. But actions often speak louder than words, so start breaking down barriers by inviting others to get educated with you.

When I first decided to go vegan overnight in August 2014, I challenged my family to join me so that we could share this unique adventure. We didn't apply any pressure to ourselves to be perfect, but only to learn as much as we could about nutritional, ethical, and environmental benefits. Each time we watched a new documentary together or tried an incredible vegan meal, our commitment became stronger . . . and so strong that it has stuck to this day! Make it relaxed and pressure-free and invite others to join your journey in the ways they wish to. If going vegan overnight seems too overwhelming for the family, casually suggest watching a documentary like *The Game Changers*, *Forks Over Knives*, *Vegucated*, or *Cowspiracy* on a movie night. Or buy super informative and approachable books such as *Vegan Reset* by Kim-Julie Hansen as a gift for people who are interested but intimidated by getting started. Get creative in how you educate, and personalize it if you need to. Maybe your family cares more about health than animals! Approach the conversation through that entry point, and the rest will follow. Even if this doesn't cause a significant change, it will increase awareness, and a curiosity that opens the door to gaining acceptance and support in your journey.

But be prepared to be tenacious, to debate and answer questions, and engage in tedious conversations. Be sure you prioritize your well-being always and try to stay relaxed and energized, because this process has the potential to be draining. Ultimately, the most important thing you can do is stay strong and true.

3. FOOD AND FLEXIBILITY

Food is one of the most prominent outlets for connection, so it's a beautiful way to bust some myths and educate as well! Whip up some of your favorite recipes from this book. Show your family and friends what all the hype is about. Instead of telling the people closest to you that plants can genuinely be delicious, let them taste it! A massive turnoff of plant-powered diets is the perception that the food is bland and one-dimensional. Prove them wrong and have fun in doing so! If you try a fantastic vegan dish or product, share your experience and give your family a taste, too. The more "normalized" plant-powered foods are, the easier it becomes to influence others to be open to eating more of them! Go out together and explore vegan restaurants near you or do a family vegan cook-off. Make the process exciting!

But what if you're not in full control of what you eat at home, or have guardians who can't fathom cooking two meals or creating special snacks or lunches? Do your best to empathize that in most families, both time and money are concerns. Kindly remind them that many "normal" dishes are already, or can be easily made, vegan (i.e., sandwiches like PB&J, granolas, pasta, soups, and so on). Share your appreciation for their effort. Offer to help or take over some parts of cooking if you can or need to. Learn some cheap, nutritious vegan meals you can make (see Eating Lively on a Budget!, page 117). Getting in the kitchen will help demonstrate your willingness to show your guardian(s) or housemates support and help them develop their own confidence in preparing plant-powered meals. This ultimately makes it easier for everyone to ease into your choices and take some of the pressure off.

Shopping can be a point of conflict. Have some troubleshooting conversations explaining what you don't eat and maybe even equip those shopping with a list to remove any chance for confusion. The heavy lifting may initially be on your end, but eventually, others will adjust to the modifications the lifestyle requires. Be flexible and understanding with yourself and others; any effort should be appreciated and celebrated. The path will be far from perfect so if you slip up here and there, don't beat yourself up. All the healthy food in the world won't make you feel better if your mind is continuously occupied by stress and worry. Your intention and effort are what counts most; don't let seeking perfection ruin the beauty of the journey.

4. GET CONNECTED

Sometimes this path can get lonely. Use the power of cultivating positive online communities and connect with others who share similar experiences. This can really help fill your cup of motivation and encouragement. Follow vegans of all backgrounds, ages, and interests to get inspired—reach out, ask questions, and exchange advice and experiences. These exchanges can really keep you going, and luckily, there are endless possibilities for connecting with plant-powered pals! And remember, I am always here to support you in your journey of Living Lively! Don't be afraid to reach out.

EATING LIVELY ON A BUDGET!

Contrary to popular belief, plant-powered diets can be some of the most in-expensive in the world. If you manage not to get carried away by shiny new vegan products at the grocery store (like I sometimes do . . . yikes!), you'll be able to get the nutrients your body needs *and* stick to your budget by purchasing real, simple whole foods. And another thing to remember: There are so many ways to eat plant-powered! You can load up on frozen meals and processed and faux foods (Oreos are vegan), eat completely clean with whole foods, or strike a balance somewhere in between. So, the money spent on eating plants depends on where you land on the spectrum and how accessible fresh fruits and vegetables are to you. Take these tips into consideration with your goals, access, and lifestyle in mind.

As I've learned to curb my grocery store shopaholic tendency (and how important it is to be *smart* with money), I've found a few hacks to save some dough while eating vegan! Here are some you can try:

$ BE A BASIC PLANT-QUEEN: KEEP IT SIMPLE AND SHOP IN BULK!

While faux foods are a ton of fun to experiment with and include in plant-powered diets from time to time, they can put a dent in your grocery budget. You don't have to give up these products entirely but should engage in mindful shopping and be aware of how often you buy them and if they are needed. For me, I know I can live without vegan meats or, and I may get a lot of backlash for this, vegan ice cream. *But* I will always and forever need oat milk and vegan cheese in my life. So, ask yourself, "Do I need that?" before purchasing veg alternatives. If the answer is no, back on the shelf it goes!

Another primary key in cutting down your grocery bill is purchasing shelf-stable staples like super filling oats and brown rice, nuts, and seeds, which are loaded with healthy fats and fiber, and protein-packed legumes in bulk (learn how to cook your beans from scratch on page 202). Legumes and grains are perfect in curries, sauces, stews, and soups for bulk cooking, and they all keep super well in the fridge and freezer. Canned foods are also an option. The nutrient-dense fruit, veg, and beans you can get in a can are as versatile and long-lasting as they are nutritious and healthful. It's these simple ingredients that are some of the healthiest options for our bodies, the planet, and our bank balances!

You can also try venturing outside of your typical grocery store and visit markets that cater to different cultures! They often have both basic and unique fresh produce that is cheaper than what you'd typically find. For example, I often find organic 99-cent canned beans at Hispanic supermarkets or more affordable tofu at Asian ones! You can also find some pretty cool sauces, spices, and grains in markets like these that can take your meals to the next level.

$ PLAN FOR GREATNESS

I spend the most money on groceries when I shop with zero plans. Without direction, it's ridiculously easy to overshop and buy things you don't need or may already have. Try to make some kind of plan before you shop for food. It doesn't have to be super concrete—I've never been into meal planning because my food moods change too often to buy for an entire week. But by having a pretty clear idea of what you want to eat for the next few days, what you have to restock on, and any specialty items you may need, you prevent overspending and food waste. That said, don't be afraid to get flexible now and then—if you see an interesting sale when you get to the store, try creating some of your meals around those discounted ingredients or products. And even better, if there are seasonal ingredients available (which are fresher and often more affordable), you can make swaps like adding squash to your curry or switching strawberries with apples in a salad.

Are you shopping with your family? Accompany the primary household shopper on their trip to the store to ensure you get what you need, or make a separate list that you can send off with them!

Bonus: If you're looking to save money and time, try challenging yourself to get in and out of the store within a specific timeframe so that you don't linger too long in the snack or dessert aisle.

$ KEEP IT SEASONAL, SWEETIE

Buying seasonal produce is a super simple way to maximize the health benefits of our food while minimizing the price! Seasonal fruit and veg are fresher and their vitamin content is greater. Seasonal produce also tends to be locally produced, which means choosing to eat seasonally supports local and sustainable farming—which significantly minimizes the environmental footprint of our food! Check out the chart of seasonal ingredients on page 130, so you can know what's currently being harvested. It's also worth taking the time to research what seasonal ingredients are available in your area specifically. You may be able to find those foods at farmers' markets, which can sell much higher-quality produce at lower prices than the grocery store. And remember: If you're looking to save money, your produce doesn't *have* to be organic. While some things, like thin-skinned foods, should be purchased organically if possible, you certainly don't have to get everything organic if you're on a budget. Pick and choose organic ingredients based on how often you use certain foods and if they are a part of the Dirty Dozen or Clean Fifteen lists (lists that determine how likely a plant is to be tainted with pesticides). Here they are (as of 2019, via the Environmental Working Group) for reference:

DIRTY DOZEN

Purchase organic if possible, or avoid until your budget permits organic (in order of highest to lowest amounts of pesticides):

* Strawberries
* Spinach
* Kale
* Nectarines
* Apples
* Grapes

* Peaches
* Cherries
* Pears
* Tomatoes
* Celery
* Potatoes

CLEAN FIFTEEN

These have little to no risk of pesticide contamination, so feel free to choose organic or conventionally grown:

* Avocados
* Sweet corn
* Pineapples
* Cabbages

* Onions
* Sweet peas (frozen)
* Papayas
* Asparagus

* Mangoes

* Eggplants

* Honeydew melons

* Kiwis

* Cantaloupes

* Cauliflower

* Broccoli

$ STAY ICY (FROZEN IS YOUR FRIEND!)

Ditch the ice on your wrist and put it in your freezer! If you want to save some cash, use frozen produce. Despite common belief, frozen fruit and veg are still super nutritious. Produce to be frozen is processed right after harvesting and packed at its freshest, so nutrient loss after picking is pretty minimal. Depending on the produce, freezing can preserve some of the nutrients and increase the availability of them in the body—sometimes more so than fresh produce, which is exposed to light, air, and varying temperatures while in transit. Another cool thing (pun intended) about buying frozen produce is that it can increase the selection of fruits and vegetables in our diets based on the wide variety we often have to choose from.

If you purchase frozen vegetables, use them within eight months. Add some olive oil and spices to frozen veggies and they will work just as well as their fresh counterparts in stews/curries, pasta dishes, stir-fries, and more. Frozen fruits should be used within about twelve months of purchase and can easily work as a stir-in for oatmeal or porridge and to make filling and nourishing smoothies or smoothie bowls.

Additionally, if you'd like, you can make your own frozen produce! Prep and freeze "ugly" or bruised fruits and vegetables (which tend to be discounted). For example, nearly rotten bananas are fantastic to buy if you know you can freeze and use them as a sweet addition to your blended creations.

All in all, fresh, frozen, and canned produce are equally affordable and nourishing—depending on the season and the type of fruit or veg. But canned or frozen produce can be more cost-effective if you are having issues with fresh food spoiling before you use it.

Many plant-powered foods keep longer than their meat- and dairy-containing counterparts, so don't be afraid to make more than you need when cooking and save for meals in the future! Most of the recipes in this book are for four people, so if you're rolling solo, these are great for nourishing your present and future self—saving both time and money! *Aaaaand*, by racking up on the leftovers, you set yourself up for another great budget-friendly strategy: bringing your own lunch to school or work or coming home to a ready-made meal. One less takeout meal = 1 hug for your bank account.

LIVING LIVELY RECIPE MODIFICATIONS

In the recipes that follow, certain ingredients called for may be less accessible or more expensive, depending on your location. But luckily, there are some easy-to-find and budget-friendly alternatives that can make for super swift swaps! If an ingredient isn't listed below, either I prefer you don't swap it or it can be

HUNGRY?

found affordably at nationwide retailers. I hope this can reduce the stress that can sometimes surround purchasing and using ingredients!

GRAINS/FLOURS

QUINOA—Swap in brown rice!

ARBORIO RICE—This type of rice can be hard to find and is more expensive compared to other varieties. The best substitutes would be grains with a good amount of starch, like sushi rice or pearl barley.

GLUTEN-FREE FLOUR—Swap in all-purpose if you don't have a gluten sensitivity or allergy.

OAT FLOUR—Make your own super cheap oat flour (see page 217)!

LIQUIDS

NUT MILKS—Use soy milk, off-brand plant milks, or shelf-stable plant milks, which tend to be much cheaper.

COCONUT WATER—Buy off-brand for lower prices!

TAMARI—If you don't have a gluten sensitivity or allergy, soy sauce will do.

PRODUCE

ARUGULA—If not available, use baby spinach leaves!

MAITAKE OR SHIITAKE MUSHROOMS—While they don't mimic the diverse flavors and textures of maitake and shiitake, button, cremini, and portobello make for great substitutes when it comes to nutrition and versatility.

NUTS

NUT BUTTERS—Swap cashew butter or almond butter (the most expensive nut butters) with their cheaper cousins, peanut butter and sunflower seed butter.

TAHINI—Tahini is crazy easy to make on your own (with just two ingredients), *and* it's cheaper than store-bought.

Homemade Tahini

MAKES ABOUT ½ CUP

1 cup hulled sesame seeds
3 to 5 tablespoons extra virgin olive oil

1. In a wide saucepan, toast the seeds over medium-low heat. No oil needed, just the dry pan. Stir constantly for 3 to 5 minutes, until the seeds are aromatic and slightly colored (not browned). Be super careful not to burn the seeds, as it can happen quickly! Transfer the toasted seeds to a large plate or baking sheet to cool thoroughly.

2. Toss them into a food processor and blend/pulse until you have a crumbly paste. Add 3 tablespoons of the oil to start and process until smooth and creamy, adding up to 2 more tablespoons oil as needed to bring the mixture to your desired consistency. Scrape the sides and process a couple seconds more.

3. Keep the homemade tahini in a container in the fridge for up to 1 month! If the oil in the tahini separates while in the refrigerator, simply stir well to fix.

SPECIALTY

VEGAN CHEESE—Some vegan cheeses are actually pretty affordable! Do some research and see what retailer might sell it inexpensively. Also, in a couple of my recipes, vegan cheese isn't a necessity. While it adds a significant amount of delicious gooeyness it isn't always a must-have . . . so no worries if you have to pass on the cheese for budget or accessibility reasons.

VEGAN YOGURT—It's usually about $1.50 to $2 for individual cups and around $5 for 24-ounce containers. Research and see if any stores near you carry the Silk, So Delicious, or Chobani brands, which are some of the more inexpensive options.

VEGAN BUTTER—Nonartisan vegan butter can range from $2 to $4 and is often worth the price! Some of the less-expensive brands that carry vegan butter include Country Crock, Pure Blends, and Earth Balance.

VEGAN MAYO—Most vegan mayo products range from $3.50 to $8 and can last quite some time, depending on the container size. They can be worth snagging if your budget permits a purchase you'd make pretty infrequently.

MISO—Miso is appealing because of the sharp, salty pop it brings to dishes. To mimic that affordably, try using soy sauce or tamari.

POWER PLUS

CHIA SEEDS—Most packages are priced around $4 to $6. Still, because chia seed products usually contain enough to go a long way, it would be worth the infrequent expenditure. You can also use sesame seeds as a substitute for their health benefits, *not* texture. In this case, it would be great for sprinkling on sweet and savory dishes. While they don't have the same amount of omega-3s as chia seeds, sesame seeds are rich in magnesium and help lower LDL ("bad") cholesterol in people who have high levels. Flaxseed meal is another great source of omega-3s that you can sprinkle on top of a dish.

BEET POWDER—Typically $4 to $8, and inexpensive if you buy it in the bulk foods department and only exactly the amount you need. But no need to stress about skipping on this if it's not available in your area.

HEMP HEARTS (HULLED HEMP SEEDS)—These go for $5 to $10 per bag and would be an infrequent investment if you'd like to add this superfood to your meals! Some cheaper ingredients with similar health benefits (heart-healthy, an excellent source of protein) include sunflower seeds, hulled pumpkin seeds, and flaxseeds.

BULLETPROOF BRAIN OCTANE OIL/MCT OIL—This specialty product isn't necessary to purchase unless you're looking for an extra energy boost and brain nourishment.

PLANT-PROTEIN POWDER—Typical containers of vegan protein powders sell for $15 to $40, and you can expect to get from 13 to 40 scoops (depending on the size and brand). When buying plant proteins, it's super important to prioritize clean ingredients—free of fillers and artificial flavoring and coloring.

GOJI BERRIES—These are usually available at natural foods stores and cost $7 to $15 per bag. For similar immunity-boosting benefits, try budget-friendly dried cranberries!

MACA POWDER—Ranging from $5 to $15, maca powder is lovely to invest in if you're looking to cope with stress. Its power lies in slowly working on the adrenal system to help the body regulate stress. The serving size is 1 teaspoon, so a container can go a long way.

SEASONINGS/FLAVORINGS

GROUND CARDAMOM—Herbal, spicy, and fragrant, cardamom is one of my favorite spices in the world, but the price of $8 or more for a 3-ounce bottle may seem unreasonable if you don't plan on using it often (like I do). But you can make your own faux cardamom: Combine equal parts ground cinnamon and either ground nutmeg, ground ginger, or ground cloves. It won't fully capture the magic of cardamom, but this combo can mimic its grounding and sweet-spicy qualities. If you want the real deal for a good deal, head to an Indian market near you.

PURE VANILLA AND ALMOND EXTRACTS—For quality almond extract, you're looking at $3 to $6, which may be feasible, as it lasts a long time and you'd use it now and then. But a bottle of pure vanilla extract (which you would use more frequently)? It's $5 to $12 and up! While I *love* me some vanilla, I often skip it in recipes to save some cash, and I avoid using the cheaper artificial vanilla flavorings, which contain chemical additives. Pure vanilla adds a beautiful pop of rich and smoky sweetness, but I personally view it as a luxe flavoring and tend to save it for special baked goods rather than breakfast foods like oatmeal. Pick and choose your usage wisely!

NUTRITIONAL YEAST—What is it, exactly? These golden flakes of goodness are made of fortified deactivated yeast and bring a nutty, cheesy flavor—plus B vitamins—to savory dishes. I use nutritional yeast often in tofu scrambles and mac 'n' cheese! It's affordable if purchased in bulk and can offset the need for vegan cheese flavorwise.

WHAT YOU NEED FOR COMPLETE KITCHEN SLAYDOM (TOOLS FOR SUCCESS)

The following lists give items and ingredients you'll generally want to have on hand when preparing recipes from this book. You'll be familiar with a lot of them already. Take count of what you've got, stock up as needed, and modify the food list to your allergies if need be.

THE LIVELY BASICS

THE MOST IMPORTANT THING
Avocado (at least to me)

SPICES AND HERBS
Chili powder (no salt added)
Chipotle powder
Dried herbs (oregano, thyme, parsley)
Garlic powder
Ground cardamom
Ground cinnamon
Ground cloves
Ground cumin
Ground nutmeg
Ground turmeric
Onion powder
Paprika

FRESH HERBS
Basil
Cilantro
Mint
Parsley
Rosemary
Thyme

GRAINS/CARBS/LEGUMES
Brown rice
Canned chickpeas, black beans, kidney beans
Corn tortillas
Fine yellow cornmeal
Oats
Pasta (my go-to brand for gluten-free pasta is Bionaturae)
Quinoa
Sandwich bread (your favorite—my go-to gluten-free and mostly vegan brand is Schär)

DRIED FRUIT/NUTS/SEEDS
Almond, peanut, or cashew butter
Cashews
Chia seeds
Coconut flakes/shredded coconut
Dates
Flaxseed meal
Golden raisins
Hemp hearts
Peanuts
Pecans
Pumpkin seeds
Slivered almonds
Sunflower seed butter
Sunflower seeds
Sesame seeds
Tahini (see page 124 to make your own)

OILS AND LIQUIDS
Clean-ingredient ketchup (I like Annie's)
Coconut oil
Extra virgin olive oil
Jamaican Scotch bonnet sauce (our family always uses Grace)
Vegetable broth (I love using Pacific Foods!)

VEGAN FAVORITES
Almond milk
Cashew milk
Full-fat and light coconut milk
Hemp milk
Nutritional yeast
Oat milk
Tempeh
Tofu

Vegan butter
Vegan shredded and sliced cheeses (Violife and Follow Your Heart are major faves!)

SWEETENERS
Agave syrup
Coconut sugar
Pure maple syrup

POWER PLUS
Beet powder
MCT oil (I use Bulletproof Brain Octane Oil)
Goji berries
Green or blue spirulina
Ground turmeric
Maca powder
Matcha powder

EXTRAS
Brown rice miso
Vegan whipped topping, coconut- or rice-based (I recommend So Delicious Coco Whip or Soyatoo! Rice Whip)
Dulse flakes
Liquid aminos
Liquid smoke
Tamari
Plant protein powder (I love using Garden of Life)
Quick-Pickled Red Onions (see page 129)

Quick-Pickled Red Onions

¾ cup rice vinegar
1 tablespoon agave
1 teaspoon kosher salt
1 teaspoon freshly ground black pepper.
1 medium red onion, thinly sliced

1. In a medium bowl, whisk the vinegar, agave, salt, and pepper with ⅓ cup water. Add the onions, stir, and let sit for 1 hour at room temperature.
2. Use immediately or store in a glass jar in the fridge for up to 3 weeks.

FRUIT AND VEG

Take special advantage of these lovely foods when they're in season! Some of these foods are available year-round, but eating seasonally is always best—for flavor, cost, and environmental reasons. Feel free to swap fruits or veggies in some recipes for a seasonal twist.

SPRING

FRUIT
Apricots
Honeydew melons
Mangoes
Oranges
Pineapples
Strawberries

VEG
Arugula
Asparagus
Beets
Bok choy
Carrots
Garlic
Herbs
Mushrooms
Onions
Peas
Potatoes
Radishes
Scallions
Spinach

SUMMER

FRUIT
Apricots
Blackberries
Blueberries
Cantaloupe
Honeydew melons
Nectarines
Peaches
Plums
Raspberries
Strawberries
Sweet and sour cherries
Watermelon

VEG
Arugula
Avocados
Beets
Chard
Corn
Cucumbers
Eggplant
Green beans
Hot and sweet peppers
Potatoes
Spinach
Squash
Tomatillos
Tomatoes

FALL AND WINTER

FRUIT
Apples
Figs
Pears
Persimmons
Pomegranates

VEG
Beets
Broccoli
Brussels sprouts
Cabbage
Carrots
Cauliflower
Fennel
Garlic
Mushrooms
Onions
Potatoes
Shallots
Sweet potatoes
Squash

EQUIPMENT AND GADGETS: THE TOOLS FOR SUCCESS

Here are some tools I recommend you have available to make your time in the kitchen a breeze:

A basic (and sharp) knife set

Cutting board(s)

Measuring cups and spoons

Whisk, spatula, flat metal spatula, wooden spoon

Baking sheets and pans

Mixing bowls (small, medium, large)

Blender (see page 179)

Food processor

Stand or hand mixer

YOU GOT THIS!

Whether you feel nervous, excited, or "nervicited" about trying these recipes, you've got this! Relax, have fun, tap into your creativity, and even break some rules. Food is all about adventure, exploration, and nourishing our bodies and souls. The more you release perfection and open up to new experiences, the more you'll enjoy cooking. Wishing you the best time ever!

Love,

Haile

good-mood
Mornings

FRUITY JAMAICAN CORNMEAL PORRIDGE

MAKES 4 SERVINGS

This is one of my favorite recipes of all time! It reminds me of weekend mornings when I'd wake up to the sweet smell of cinnamon and run downstairs to find my dad whisking a big pot of authentic Jamaican porridge. While incredibly simple, this dish is one that really connects me to my roots. I'll always cherish the times I spent slurping up a huge bowl of porridge and listening to my dad recount his childhood in Jamaica. It's a special occasion when my dad makes porridge . . . because it's literally the only thing he knows how to make. But he sure has it mastered!

3 cups unsweetened plant milk of your choice, plus more if desired

2 cups canned light coconut milk (about 1⅓ 13.5-ounce cans)

1 cup fine yellow cornmeal

1 to 2 teaspoons ground cinnamon, to taste

¼ teaspoon ground nutmeg

½ cup pure maple syrup or liquid sweetener of your choice

OPTIONAL (BUT HIGHLY RECOMMENDED) TOPPINGS

Sliced Bosc pears

Blueberries

Raspberries

1. In a medium saucepan, combine the plant milk and coconut milk. Bring to a boil over medium-high heat. Gradually whisk in the cornmeal, then reduce the heat to medium, continuing to whisk to prevent lumps from forming. Cook for 5 minutes, or until thickened.

2. Add the cinnamon, nutmeg, and maple syrup and whisk to combine. Adjust the consistency with extra plant milk if desired.

3. Remove from the heat, top with your favorite fruit (if using), and dig in with the people you love!

MCFLUFFY TOFU BREAKFAST SANDWICHES

MAKES 4 SERVINGS

I can vividly remember picking up breakfast on the way to school when I was really little, excitedly going through the drive-thru, and then scarfing down a bacon, egg, and cheese sandwich in complete bliss. I wanted to re-create that bliss with a breakfast sandwich that is happy dance–inducing, layered, a little messy, and so much more nutritious. There's no stopping you when you start the day with this!

TEMPEH BACON

1 tablespoon tamari or liquid aminos
1 tablespoon pure maple syrup
1 teaspoon liquid smoke
1 teaspoon chili powder
1 teaspoon garlic powder
Freshly ground black pepper
2 tablespoons olive oil
One 8-ounce package tempeh, cut into ¼-inch-thick slices

FLUFFY TOFU

One 14-ounce package extra-firm tofu
1 tablespoon nutritional yeast
1 teaspoon garlic powder

1 teaspoon ground turmeric
½ teaspoon freshly ground black pepper
Salt
2 teaspoons olive oil
4 slices vegan cheddar cheese (optional but highly recommended)

SANDWICHES

8 slices your favorite bread (I love using ciabatta or sourdough!)
4 slices beefsteak tomato
1 cup loosely packed arugula
8 fresh basil leaves, thinly sliced
1 avocado, sliced or mashed

1. To make the tempeh bacon: In a small bowl, combine the tamari, maple syrup, liquid smoke, chili powder, garlic powder, pepper, and 1 tablespoon of the olive oil. Set aside.

2. In a large skillet, heat the remaining 1 tablespoon olive oil over medium heat. Add the tempeh and cook for 2 minutes on each side, until golden brown and crisp.

3. Pour the tamari/spice mixture over the tempeh, making sure all the strips are coated. Cook 2 to 3 minutes, until heated through. Remove the tempeh from the skillet and set aside.

4. To make the fluffy tofu: Drain the tofu and gently squeeze it with paper towels to soak up any excess liquid. Cut the tofu block into eight ¾- to 1-inch-thick slices and set aside.

5. In a small bowl, combine the nutritional yeast, garlic powder, turmeric, pepper, and salt to taste. Sprinkle the spice mixture evenly over both sides of the tofu.

6. In the same skillet used to cook the tempeh, heat the olive oil over high heat. When the pan is hot, lay the seasoned tofu slices in the pan in a single layer. Cook for 1 to 2 minutes, then gently flip the tofu slices, reduce the heat to medium, cover, and cook for 3 minutes, until the tofu is slightly puffed and fluffy. Flip the slices once more; they should be golden brown with a light crust.

7. If you're using cheese, break each slice in half and place it on top of a tofu slice. Cover and cook for about 2 minutes to fully melt the cheese. Set the pan aside, covered.

8. To assemble the sandwiches: Toast the bread. For each sandwich, layer 2 slices of tofu, a beefsteak tomato slice, a handful of fresh arugula, a pinch of basil, and the tempeh bacon. Top with avocado slices.

9. Serve and enjoy this grown-up remix of a classic!

GOLDEN DREAM TURMERIC-BERRY CHIA PUDDING

MAKES 2 TO 4 SERVINGS

It's nice to bring a little magic into our mornings every now and then! Chia seeds are fantastic for keeping you full and energized, while powerful ingredients like turmeric and berries help to reduce inflammation and give your immune system a boost. This chia pudding is the perfect grab-and-go breakfast that'll put a little pep in your morning step.

TURMERIC LAYER

½ cup full-fat coconut milk
½ cup plant-based yogurt of your choice (I usually use coconut or almond!)
2 tablespoons chia seeds
2 tablespoons pure maple syrup or liquid sweetener of your choice
1 teaspoon pure vanilla extract
1 teaspoon ground turmeric
½ teaspoon ground cinnamon
Pinch of freshly ground black pepper
Pinch of ground nutmeg

BERRY LAYER

½ cup full-fat coconut milk
½ cup plant-based yogurt of your choice
2 tablespoons pure maple syrup or liquid sweetener of your choice
½ cup raspberries
1 teaspoon pure vanilla extract
½ teaspoon ground cinnamon
2 tablespoons chia seeds
Power Plus: Add 1 teaspoon beet powder for a brain boost!

OPTIONAL (BUT HIGHLY RECOMMENDED) TOPPINGS

Blueberries/strawberries/sliced banana
Power Plus: Add hemp hearts for protein and more fiber!

1. To make the turmeric layer: In a medium bowl, stir together the coconut milk, yogurt, chia seeds, maple syrup, vanilla, turmeric, cinnamon, black pepper, and nutmeg. Cover and set aside.

2. To make the berry layer: In a food processor, combine the coconut milk, yogurt, maple syrup, raspberries, vanilla, and cinnamon and process until fully blended. Pour into a medium bowl, add the chia seeds, and stir well.

3. Cover and place both pudding layers in the fridge. Let set overnight.

4. In the morning, make your bowls, creating layers however you like— turmeric on top of berry, berry on top of turmeric—you decide! If desired, top with fresh fruit and hemp hearts and serve.

BLENDER OATS

MAKES 4 SERVINGS

One morning I was bored and decided to put my oats in the blender. The rest is delicious history. Pulsing oats with some crunchy and chewy ingredients adds a nice layer to a breakfast staple that can easily become pretty boring and repetitive.

2½ cups unsweetened oat milk, plus ½ cup to blend in

2 cups light coconut milk (about 1⅓ 13.5-ounce cans)

2½ cups quick-cooking oats (gluten-free if needed)

½ to 1 cup coconut sugar, to taste

2 teaspoons pure vanilla extract

¼ teaspoon ground cardamom

½ cup unsweetened shredded coconut

½ cup sliced almonds or nuts of your choice

¼ cup raw pumpkin seeds

½ cup dried cherries or golden raisins

Power Plus: Add 1 tablespoon MCT oil for brain nourishment!

OPTIONAL (BUT HIGHLY RECOMMENDED) TOPPINGS

Fresh berries

Nut/seed butter

Melted vegan chocolate

1. In a medium saucepan, combine the oat and coconut milks and bring to a steady boil over medium heat. Add the oats and stir to combine. Cook for 5 minutes, or until the oats have softened and thickened.

2. Transfer the oatmeal to a blender (high-powered, if possible) and add the rest of the ingredients and the ½ cup oat milk. Pulse 3 to 5 times, until the seeds and nuts are slightly broken down. You want the blended oats to have a diverse texture, with a balance of crunchiness, smoothness, and chewiness.

3. Divide the oats among four bowls. If desired, top with any berries, nut/seed butter, and chocolate you'd like!

CHAI-COCONUT BANANA BREAD
FRENCH TOAST STICKS

MAKES 4 SERVINGS

This recipe is ridiculously simple when you do some prepping the night before. Make the banana bread, resist eating it all warm out of the oven (but do sneak a bite—I won't tell!), and refrigerate overnight. In the morning, cut the banana bread into sticks and soak them in a rich coconut milk batter. Pan-fry them to perfection!

½ cup full-fat coconut milk
½ cup unsweetened oat milk
2 tablespoons pure maple syrup
1 teaspoon pure vanilla extract
¼ cup cornstarch or arrowroot
1 tablespoon nutritional yeast
1 tablespoon oat flour, store-bought or homemade (page 217)
1 teaspoon ground cinnamon
Pinch of sea salt
4 to 6 tablespoons vegan butter

Gluten-Free Chai-Coconut Banana Bread (page 241), halved lengthwise, then cut crosswise into about 12 "sticks"

OPTIONAL (BUT HIGHLY RECOMMENDED) TOPPINGS
Seasonal fruits (see chart on page 130 for ideas)
Pure maple syrup
Vegan chocolate chips
Vegan whipped topping (I recommend So Delicious Coco Whip or Soyatoo! Rice Whip)

1. To make the batter, in a large bowl, whisk together the coconut milk, oat milk, maple syrup, vanilla, cornstarch, nutritional yeast, oat flour, cinnamon, and salt.

2. In a large skillet, melt some of the vegan butter over medium-high heat. Dip the banana bread slices into the batter, flipping to coat both sides. Don't oversaturate the bread, as it will become soggy and fall apart. Work in batches so that you coat only as many slices of bread as fit into the pan at once without crowding. Lay the sticks in the pan and cook for about 5 minutes on each side, until golden brown, using a spatula to flip them carefully. Add more vegan butter as needed between batches.

3. If desired, top with seasonal fruit and a drizzle of maple syrup! If you wanna go crazy, enjoy with chocolate chips and some whipped topping. :)

GLUTEN-FREE SUNDAY MORNING HERB BISCUITS

MAKES 12 BISCUITS (TO SERVE 4 TO 6)

My favorite day to have breakfast is Sunday. Since I was little, my family has loved to make breakfast spreads on as many Sundays as possible. It's our day to slow down, treat ourselves, and refuel for the week ahead. Before going vegan (and gluten-free), my favorite parts of the breakfast spread were 1,000 percent the biscuits. Out of the can, but fluffy, buttery, flaky, and just absolute heaven, to be honest. This biscuit recipe has come the closest to re-creating that happiness . . . with a gluten-free twist!

1 cup plus 2 tablespoons unsweetened oat milk
1 tablespoon distilled white vinegar
2 cups Bob's Red Mill Gluten-Free 1 to 1 Baking Flour or other 1:1 gluten-free flour
¼ cup cornstarch
2 tablespoons coconut sugar
1 tablespoon baking powder
½ teaspoon baking soda
1 tablespoon garlic powder or ½ tablespoon minced fresh garlic
1 tablespoon fresh thyme leaves
¾ teaspoon fine sea salt
6 tablespoons (¾ stick) vegan butter, chilled, plus 2 tablespoons vegan butter, melted
Vegan butter, at room temperature, and/or jam of your choice, for serving

1. Preheat the oven to 400°F. Line a baking sheet with parchment paper.

2. In a small bowl, combine the oat milk and vinegar. Set aside.

3. In a large bowl, whisk the flour, cornstarch, coconut sugar, baking powder, baking soda, garlic, thyme, and salt until well combined. Add the chilled vegan butter. Using a fork or your fingers (I always use my fingers!), smush the butter into the flour mixture until only little pieces remain. The mixture should resemble coarse crumbs.

4. Pour the oat milk/vinegar mixture into the flour mixture and mix gently with a spoon until fully combined.

5. Use an ice cream scoop to scoop balls of the biscuit dough onto the prepared sheet pan. You will get about 12 balls. Lightly press down on the tops of the dough and brush with the melted vegan butter.

6. Bake for 15 to 17 minutes, until the tops are golden brown. Remove to a rack to let cool for 10 to 15 minutes.

7. Enjoy with butter, jam, or as part of your Sunday morning breakfast spread. :)

NUTTY QUINOA PARFAIT

MAKES 4 SERVINGS

I hopped on the quinoa wave around 2012 and basically never hopped off. Quinoa is incredibly nutritious and versatile; I love using it in sweet dishes to mix things up and get in a high-fiber, high-protein breakfast. Here the quinoa mix of dried fruit and almonds acts kind of like a soft granola. I love when getting in this much goodness is super easy!

2 cups cooked quinoa (cooked according to package instructions)
1 cup raw slivered almonds or your favorite nut/seed
½ cup golden raisins (chopped dates, dried apricots, and dried cherries are all great subs!)
2 tablespoons pure maple syrup
2 teaspoons pure vanilla extract
2 teaspoons ground cinnamon

2 cups coconut-milk yogurt or your favorite plant-based yogurt

OPTIONAL (BUT HIGHLY RECOMMENDED) TOPPINGS
Power Plus: hemp hearts
Power Plus: chia seeds
Seasonal fruits (see chart on page 130 for ideas)

1. In a food processor, combine the quinoa, almonds, raisins, maple syrup, vanilla, and cinnamon and pulse 3 to 5 times, until the almonds are slightly crushed and the ingredients are lightly incorporated. The quinoa should still retain most of its texture.

2. Place ½ cup yogurt and ½ cup quinoa mix in each of four bowls. If desired, top with seeds and seasonal fruit. Enjoy as the perfect way to start your day!

FRENCH TOAST WITH CRISPY OVEN-FRIED MUSHROOMS

MAKES 4 SERVINGS

I like to think of this recipe as a "morning project."—something special that I can dig my hands and time into. If you get into these morning moods, too, or just want to try a super fun and unique breakfast dish, this is for you. The incredibly delicious crispy mushrooms will take most of the time, so get those going and baking in the oven, and then jump to the French toast. Set aside a bit of time and get lost in it!

BATTER

½ cup full-fat coconut milk
½ cup unsweetened oat milk
2 tablespoons pure maple syrup
1 teaspoon pure vanilla extract
¼ cup cornstarch
1 tablespoon oat flour, store-bought or homemade (see page 217)
1 tablespoon nutritional yeast
2 tablespoons fresh thyme leaves

FRENCH TOAST AND FIXINGS

2 to 4 tablespoons vegan butter
4 to 6 slices of your favorite bread (preferably a softer variety)
2 to 6 tablespoons fruit jam of your choice (I highly recommend a berry flavor)
Oven-Fried Mushrooms (page 197)
Pure maple syrup

1. To make the batter: In a large bowl, whisk together the coconut milk, oat milk, maple syrup, vanilla, cornstarch, oat flour, nutritional yeast, and thyme.

2. To make the French toast: Heat a large skillet over medium-high heat and melt some of the vegan butter. Dip each slice of bread into the batter, flipping to coat the other side. Don't oversaturate the bread as it will become soggy and fall apart. Work in batches so that you coat only as many slices of bread as fit into the pan at once without crowding.

3. Cook the French toast for about 5 minutes on each side, until golden brown. Add more vegan butter as needed between batches.

4. Spread ½ to 1 tablespoon jam over each slice of toast. Place a mushroom piece or two on top and drizzle with maple syrup. Savor this funky breakfast indulgence!

CHOCOLATE-GINGER-STRAWBERRY OAT BARS

MAKES 4 SERVINGS

This recipe has saved me on *so* many busy mornings! As someone who is pretty much always on the go, I need something hearty I can grab before hopping in the car or on a train or plane. The strawberry, chocolate, ginger, and orange are a delightful combo, and the oat base keeps me full and energized.

CRUST AND CRUMBLE

6 tablespoons coconut oil or vegan butter, melted
1½ cups Bob's Red Mill Gluten-Free 1 to 1 Baking Flour or other 1:1 gluten-free flour
2 tablespoons unsweetened cocoa powder
1½ cups rolled oats (gluten-free if needed)
½ cup pure maple syrup
2 teaspoons pure vanilla extract
2 to 4 teaspoons grated fresh ginger, to taste
¼ cup golden coconut sugar
1 tablespoon ground cinnamon
Pinch of kosher salt

STRAWBERRY FILLING

1½ cups sliced strawberries
½ tablespoon fresh lemon juice
1 teaspoon pure vanilla extract
1 teaspoon Bob's Red Mill Gluten-Free 1 to 1 Baking Flour or other 1:1 gluten-free flour
2 tablespoons grated orange zest

1. Preheat the oven to 350°F. Line the bottom of an 8-inch square baking dish with parchment paper.

2. To make the crust and crumble: In a large bowl, mix together the coconut oil, flour, cocoa, oats, maple syrup, vanilla, ginger, sugar, cinnamon, and salt until well combined but still slightly crumbly.

3. Measure out ½ cup of the mixture and set aside for the crumble topping. Place the remaining mixture in the prepared pan and spread it out evenly across the bottom with your fingers.

4. To make the strawberry filling: In a small bowl, mix together the strawberries, lemon juice, vanilla, flour, and orange zest. Spread the strawberry mixture evenly over the crust.

5. Sprinkle the reserved crumble evenly over the strawberry layer. Bake for 50 minutes, until golden brown and toasty. Cool for 25 to 30 minutes.

6. Cut, serve, and enjoy! Refrigerate them for up to 3 days.

MAKE-IT-YOUR-OWN (MIYO) TOFU SCRAMBLE

MAKES 4 SERVINGS

I used to be such an egghead and would eat scrambled eggs nearly every morning. When I went vegan, I wanted to make sure I could mimic my creamy and cheesy scrambles with more good-for-you ingredients—with no little chicks (or mamas) harmed in the making. Nutritional yeast adds a rich and nutty "cheesy" flavor, while the layering of herbs, spices, and add-ins really brings the scramble to life! And sometimes, when I'm looking to amplify the experience, I'll add a pinch or two of black salt (aka *kala namak*), which emulates the sulfuric taste in eggs.

One 14-ounce package extra-firm tofu, drained
1 teaspoon garlic powder
1 teaspoon dried oregano
1 teaspoon fresh or dried thyme
5 tablespoons nutritional yeast
1 tablespoon olive oil
½ yellow onion, cut into medium dice
Kosher salt
¼ cup unsweetened oat milk
½ cup shredded vegan cheese of your choice

OPTIONAL (BUT HIGHLY RECOMMENDED) ADD-INS
Greens: chopped kale/spinach/Swiss chard
Halved cherry tomatoes
Chopped fresh cilantro
Chopped fresh parsley
Pinch of black salt (kala namak)
Minced chives
Sliced scallions
Microgreen of your choice (I love pea shoots!)

1. In a medium bowl, smash the tofu until it's soft but still a bit chunky. Set aside.

2. In a small bowl, combine the garlic powder, oregano, thyme, and 3 tablespoons of the nutritional yeast.

3. In a large skillet, heat the olive oil over medium heat. Add the onion and sauté for 2 minutes, or until softened.

4. In a small bowl, mix the remaining 2 tablespoons nutritional yeast with ¼ cup water. Add to the pan and stir to incorporate. Add the spice blend, salt to taste, the oat milk, and the vegan cheese and stir to combine.

5. Increase the heat to medium-high and cook, stirring occasionally, for 5 minutes to meld the flavors and melt the cheese. Taste and adjust the flavors and salt as needed.

6. Reduce the heat and mix in any additional ingredients, like veggies and fresh herbs. Remove from the heat and serve!

CHICKPEA-POWER PANCAKES

MAKES 4 SERVINGS

Chickpea flour makes these pancakes incredibly soft, fluffy, and full of protein and fiber. Go crazy with the toppings for a new experience every time you dig into these tasty lil cakes!

1 cup chickpea flour
1 teaspoon ground cinnamon
1 teaspoon baking powder
¾ cup unsweetened oat milk
1½ tablespoons pure maple syrup
1 teaspoon pure vanilla extract
1 vegan egg (I use Bob's Red Mill Gluten Free Vegan Egg Replacer)
1 teaspoon apple cider vinegar
Coconut oil, for the pan

OPTIONAL (BUT HIGHLY RECOMMENDED) TOPPINGS
Seasonal fruits (see chart on page 130 for ideas)
Maple syrup
Chopped nuts/seeds
Vegan yogurt
Nut butter
Melted vegan chocolate

1. In a medium bowl, whisk together the chickpea flour, cinnamon, and baking powder. Add the oat milk, maple syrup, vanilla, vegan egg, and vinegar and whisk until fully incorporated. (See Tip.)

2. In a large skillet, melt about 1 tablespoon of coconut oil over medium heat. Scoop about 2 tablespoons batter per pancake into the pan. To avoid over-crowding the pan, cook no more than 4 pancakes at a time.

3. Cover the pan and steam the pancakes for 2 minutes on each side. Uncover, flip, and cook for 1 minute. Flip again and cook for 30 to 60 seconds. Remove the pancakes from the pan and repeat to make the rest of the pancakes, adding more coconut oil to the pan as needed.

4. Top with anything you'd like! I love simple toppings, like berries, maple syrup, and coconut, or decadent ones, such as cinnamon-cashew butter and chocolate. :)

Tip: Don't taste the batter! The chickpea flour has a distinct savory flavor that only goes away after cooking/steaming. It'll be worth the wait!

Craveable
Combos

MAKE-IT-YOUR-OWN (MIYO) OVERNIGHT OATS GUIDE

MAKES 2 OR 3 SERVINGS

I personally love making overnight oats because I can use my base recipe and completely build it out from there with unique and fun flavor and ingredient combos. I often eat it as a filling and nourishing to-go snack or breakfast when I'm really busy. And because I love you, just know that while it's a great meal for on the go, it isn't the best snack to bring to the airport. TSA will snatch your overnight oats *and* your jar and toss both into the trash without batting an eye. RIP to my favorite Pumpkin Spice Oats—I'm still upset about it!! My love-hate relationship with TSA aside, below you'll find a super simple guide to help you create an overnight oats base that you love and can play around with to make your own! And you can check out three of my favorite recipes for some inspiration.

INGREDIENTS YOU'LL NEED

Oats: I highly recommend using old-fashioned rolled oats for the best consistency! And use gluten-free oats if you need to. :)

Chia seeds: These seeds help give the overnight oats a pudding-like texture. Plus, they're packed with fiber, iron, and calcium, to name a few!

Vegan yogurt: I love using vegan yogurt in my overnight oats because it adds an element of creaminess. Coconut-milk and almond-milk yogurt are my personal go-tos . . . but you can use any kind you prefer.

Plant milk: Any plant milk works here! Some of my favorites are oat, hemp, and, for richer overnight oats, full-fat coconut milk.

Pure vanilla extract (optional): I think vanilla makes every sweet thing better! Add some for a pop and to enhance the flavor of your overnight oats.

Liquid sweetener: My go-to is pure maple syrup, but you do you!

Mix-ins and toppings: Diced or mashed fruit, purees, nut butters, spices, superfood powders . . . have some fun with this! Play around with different ratios and combos to see what you like.

What to Do

Start with the suggested ratio below and add more or less milk or yogurt to get the consistency that's just right for you. Once you master the basic overnight oats recipe, there's no limit to the diverse flavor and topping combos!

Step 1

1 cup rolled oats + 1 tablespoon chia seeds + ½ cup vegan yogurt + 1 cup plant milk + 1 teaspoon pure vanilla extract + 1 tablespoon liquid sweetener + any mix-ins!

In a medium bowl, combine the oats, chia seeds, yogurt, milk, vanilla, sweetener, and mix-ins and mix until the oats are smooth, with no clumps. Don't be afraid to go off on this part; play around with spice and mix-in combos to discover a new favorite!

Step 2

Seal or cover the oat mixture with a lid and refrigerate for at least 2 to 3 hours or overnight.

Step 3

In a few hours or the next morning, remove the oats from the fridge and divide among two or three jars or bowls. Add some fresh toppings if you wish and dig in! :)

PUMPKIN PIE OVERNIGHT OATS

MAKES 2 OR 3 SERVINGS

If you wish you could eat like it's autumn in summer or spring, these pumpkin pie overnight oats are a nice way to bring in those warm and comfy holiday flavors any day!

OVERNIGHT OATS

1 cup rolled oats (gluten-free if needed)
1 tablespoon chia seeds
½ cup coconut-milk yogurt
1 cup unsweetened oat milk
⅔ cup canned unsweetened pumpkin puree
1 teaspoon pure vanilla extract
2 tablespoons pure maple syrup
2 tablespoons hemp hearts

1 teaspoon ground cinnamon
1 teaspoon ground ginger
Pinch of ground nutmeg

OPTIONAL (BUT HIGHLY RECOMMENDED) TOPPINGS

Golden Milk Granola (page 161)
Seasonal fruits (see chart on page 130 for ideas)

1. To make the overnight oats: In a medium bowl, combine all the ingredients. Cover and refrigerate overnight.

2. In the morning, divide the oats among two or three jars or bowls and top with granola and fruits, if desired.

BERRY-CHERRY-COCONUT OVERNIGHT OATS

MAKES 2 OR 3 SERVINGS

If you're into sweetness with a little tang, this is a fun combo that I make when I'm craving something with layers of fruitiness!

OVERNIGHT OATS

1 cup rolled oats (gluten-free if needed)
1 tablespoon chia seeds
½ cup coconut-milk yogurt
1 cup unsweetened oat milk
1 teaspoon pure vanilla extract
1 tablespoon pure maple syrup
1 small banana, mashed
½ cup slightly mashed blueberries
¼ cup slightly mashed raspberries
½ cup diced cherries

OPTIONAL (BUT HIGHLY RECOMMENDED) TOPPINGS

Coconut cream
Raspberries and/or cherries
Bananas
Pure maple syrup

1. To make the overnight oats: In a medium bowl, combine all the ingredients. Cover and refrigerate overnight.

2. In the morning, divide the oats among two or three jars or bowls. If desired, top with coconut cream, raspberries and/or cherries, and a touch of maple syrup. Enjoy!

CARROT CAKE OVERNIGHT OATS

MAKES 2 OR 3 SERVINGS

I *looove* carrot cake with my whole soul. This recipe is a great way to eat "cake" for breakfast without really eating cake for breakfast. ;)

1 cup rolled oats (gluten-free if needed)
1 tablespoon chia seeds
½ cup coconut-milk yogurt
1 cup full-fat coconut milk
1 teaspoon pure vanilla extract
2 tablespoons pure maple syrup
1 carrot, peeled and grated
¼ cup golden raisins
¼ cup unsweetened shredded coconut
Dash of ground cardamom

OPTIONAL (BUT HIGHLY RECOMMENDED) TOPPINGS

Walnuts
Pecans
Unsweetened coconut flakes
Seasonal fruits (see chart on page 130 for ideas)

1. To make the overnight oats: In a medium bowl, combine all the ingredients. Cover and refrigerate overnight.

2. In the morning, divide the oats among two or three jars or bowls and top with nuts and fruits, if desired.

MAKE-IT-YOUR-OWN (MIYO) GRANOLA GUIDE

MAKES 4 TO 8 CUPS

I've always had a special place in my heart for granola. Playing around with chewy and crunchy textures, layered spices, and flavor pairings makes the possibilities endless! I love eating my granola like cereal with plant milk, in a bowl with plant yogurt, layered in an overnight oat jar, on top of desserts, or simply on its own. Refer to the guide below to help you build the perfect granola. And don't miss out on three of my favorite combos that follow!

INGREDIENTS YOU'LL NEED

Oats: I recommend using rolled oats! They provide just the right amount of creamy and chewy texture. Use gluten-free oats if you need to. :)

Nuts and seeds: They add great crunchy texture and bulk to the granola, as well as a nutrient boost of fiber, healthy fats, protein, and heart-lovin' vitamins and minerals.

Dried fruit: Great for added flavor, texture, fiber, and antioxidants. While it can be wonderful for adding a nice dimension of chewiness to granola, some dried fruit can be loaded with unnatural sugars and preservatives. Try your best to read labels and use no-sugar-added fruit with ingredients you can pronounce!

Coconut sugar: This is my go-to sweetener because it adds a nice nutty coconut flavor and is more nutrient- and fiber-dense than white or brown sugar.

Spices and zests: Experimenting with spices can help you create unique and harmonious flavor combos . . . and even add additional health benefits! And I love adding citrus zests to make my granola pop.

Liquids: The holy trinity: coconut oil, pure maple syrup, and pure vanilla extract.

What to Do

Start with the suggested ratio opposite and experiment with different ratios of nuts and seeds to dried fruit if you'd like! Of course, you can have some fun with the spices and even try different extracts to add a diverse pop of flavor (culinary rose extract is lovely!).

Step 1

Preheat the oven to 350°F. Line a large sheet pan with parchment paper.

Step 2

2 cups rolled oats + up to 6 cups total of nuts/coconut flakes/dried fruit or chewy ingredients (such as crystallized ginger) + ¼ cup seeds of your choice + 1 tablespoon coconut sugar + 1 teaspoon Himalayan pink salt + spices (start with up to 2 teaspoons of spices and adjust from there)

In a large bowl, combine all the dry ingredients. Set aside.

Step 3

¼ cup melted coconut oil + ½ cup pure maple syrup + 1 teaspoon pure vanilla extract (or a fun extract like coffee, orange, or rose)

In a small bowl, combine all the liquid ingredients.

Step 4

Pour the liquid mixture over the dry ingredients and incorporate well with your hands or a spoon. Spread the granola mix in an even layer on the prepared sheet pan. (Optional: Drizzle 1 to 2 tablespoons extra maple syrup on top of the granola.)

Step 5

Bake for 20 minutes, or until golden brown. Let cool for 30 minutes before serving. Devour as a snack, cereal, or layer in a plant-based parfait! Store in an airtight container for up to 7 days.

GOLDEN MILK GRANOLA

MAKES 4 CUPS

This was one of the first granola recipes I ever made (and it's still one of my favorites!). I'm obsessed with the golden milk drink because of its heart-healthiness and brain- and mood-boosting benefits (it makes me feel so cozy and grounded!) and wanted to bring its warm spiciness to my snack and breakfast meals. Make this granola if you want to brighten and spice up the start to your day!

2 cups rolled oats (gluten-free if needed)
2 cups chopped raw pecans
2 cups unsweetened coconut flakes
¼ cup chia seeds
1 tablespoon coconut sugar
1 cup golden raisins
½ cup small diced crystallized ginger
1 teaspoon Himalayan pink salt
1 teaspoon ground cinnamon

½ teaspoon ground nutmeg
¼ teaspoon ground allspice
¼ teaspoon ground cardamom
Pinch of freshly ground black pepper

LIQUID INGREDIENTS

¼ cup coconut oil, melted
½ cup pure maple syrup
1 teaspoon pure vanilla extract

1. Preheat the oven to 350°F. Line a large sheet pan with parchment paper.

2. In a large bowl, combine the oats, pecans, coconut flakes, chia seeds, coconut sugar, raisins, ginger, salt, and spices. Set aside.

3. In a small bowl, combine the coconut oil, maple syrup, and vanilla. Pour this mixture over the dry ingredients and incorporate well with your hands or a spoon.

4. Spread the granola mix in one even layer on the prepared sheet pan. (Optional: Drizzle 1 to 2 tablespoons more maple syrup over the granola.)

5. Bake for 20 minutes, or until golden brown.

6. Let cool for 30 minutes before serving. Devour as a snack or cereal or layer in a plant-based parfait! Store in an airtight container for up to 7 days.

BERRY CITRUS GRANOLA

MAKES 6 CUPS

My favorite thing about this granola is the irresistible pop of zesty lemon and sweet tanginess of the berries! It's fun, fresh, and fruity . . . which is the vibe I always aspire to have.

2 cups rolled oats (gluten-free if needed)
2 cups chopped raw cashews
1 cup unsweetened coconut flakes
½ cup raw pumpkin seeds
¼ cup chia seeds
1 tablespoon coconut sugar
2 cups dried blueberries
1 teaspoon Himalayan pink salt
1 teaspoon ground cinnamon

LIQUID INGREDIENTS

¼ cup coconut oil, melted
½ cup pure maple syrup
1 teaspoon pure vanilla extract

1 to 2 tablespoons grated lemon zest, to taste
1 cup freeze-dried strawberries

1. Preheat the oven to 350°F. Line a large sheet pan with parchment paper.

2. In a large bowl, combine the oats, cashews, coconut flakes, pumpkin seeds, chia seeds, coconut sugar, dried blueberries, salt, and cinnamon. (Don't add the strawberries just yet!) Set aside.

3. In a small bowl, combine the coconut oil, maple syrup, vanilla, and lemon zest. Pour this mixture over the granola ingredients and incorporate well with your hands or a spoon.

4. Spread the granola mix in one even layer on the prepared sheet pan. (Optional: Drizzle 1 to 2 tablespoons more maple syrup over the granola.)

5. Bake for 20 minutes, or until golden brown.

6. Let cool for 30 minutes, then toss in the strawberries. Devour as a snack or cereal or layer in a plant-based parfait! Store in an airtight container for up to 7 days.

APRICOT SUNSHINE GRANOLA

MAKES 8 CUPS

The combo of seeds, nuts, and sweet, chewy apricots makes for a hearty granola that can be paired with anything or enjoyed simply on its own!

2 cups rolled oats (gluten-free if needed)
2 cups chopped raw almonds
2 cups unsweetened coconut flakes
½ cup hulled sunflower seeds
¼ cup sesame seeds
1 tablespoon coconut sugar
1 cup chopped dried apricots
1 teaspoon Himalayan pink salt

1 teaspoon ground cinnamon
½ teaspoon ground nutmeg

LIQUID INGREDIENTS
¼ cup coconut oil, melted
½ cup pure maple syrup
1 teaspoon pure vanilla extract

2 tablespoons grated orange zest

1. Preheat the oven to 350°F. Line a large sheet pan with parchment paper.

2. In a large bowl, combine the oats, almonds, coconut flakes, sunflower seeds, sesame seeds, coconut sugar, apricots, salt, and spices. Set aside.

3. In a small bowl, combine the coconut oil, maple syrup, vanilla, and orange zest. Pour this mixture over the granola ingredients and incorporate well with your hands or a spoon.

4. Spread the granola mix in one even layer on the prepared sheet pan. (Optional: Drizzle 1 to 2 tablespoons more maple syrup over the granola.)

5. Bake for 20 minutes, or until golden brown.

6. Let cool for 30 minutes before serving. Devour as a snack or cereal or layer in a plant-based parfait! Store in an airtight container for up to 7 days.

NEXT-LEVEL TOASTS

Toast is probably the *most* basic yet flexible food out there. Whether you want to keep it simple with some PB or bring it to the next level with sweet potato mash and roasted apples, the possibilities are endless. I challenge you to let loose and allow your bread to be a canvas for creativity and all kinds of exciting flavor mash-ups. Check out the guide below for some pointers on what components can be combined to make an out-of-this-world toast.

Try the following three recipes to inspire you to dream bigger than your plain slice of bread!

Keys to next-level toasts

INTERESTING SPREADS	STAPLE TOPPINGS	SPRINKLES AND DRIZZLES
Hummus—beet, pesto, roasted pepper	**Seasonal fruits and veg**—raw or roasted—check out what's in season and use those ingredients for max flavor!	**Nuts and seeds**—coconut flakes, sesame seeds, pumpkin seeds, hemp hearts, chia seeds
Mashes and purees—avocado, pumpkin, butternut, sweet potato	**Proteins**—tofu, tempeh, legumes	**Dried fruit**—golden raisins, cranberries, apricots, dates
Smashed beans—black beans, chickpeas, white beans		**Nut and seed butters**—sunflower seed, almond, cashew, peanut, hazelnut
Jams and nut butters—apricot or pineapple jam, cashew or pecan butter		**Nondairy cheeses**—shreds, creamy spreads, slices
Green Queen Dipping Sauce (page 238) makes for an epic spread as well!		**Herbs and spices**—fresh thyme or rosemary, paprika, cayenne, curry powder

PURPLE SWEET POTATO AND APPLE TOAST

MAKES 4 SERVINGS

I love everything about fall—the flavors, the weather, the cute sweaters, the smell of cinnamon in the air. And I can teleport right into my favorite season through the special combo of cozy and warming ingredients slathered and piled onto this toast.

PURPLE SWEET POTATO SPREAD
1 medium purple or regular sweet potato
1 tablespoon pure maple syrup
½ teaspoon ground ginger
½ teaspoon ground cinnamon

CINNAMON APPLES
2 medium Honeycrisp apples, cored and cut into medium dice
2 tablespoons coconut sugar
1 teaspoon pure vanilla extract

1 teaspoon ground cinnamon
½ teaspoon kosher salt
1 tablespoon solid coconut oil

TOASTS
4 slices bread of your choice, toasted
Almond butter
Raw pumpkin seeds
Unsweetened shredded coconut
Pure maple syrup

1. Preheat the oven to 400°F. Line a sheet pan with parchment paper.

2. To make the purple sweet potato spread: Pierce the sweet potato 4 or 5 times with a fork and wrap it in foil. Place it on the oven rack and bake for 30 to 40 minutes, until soft. When cool, peel and mash the potato. Measure out ½ cup of mashed sweet potato and place in a medium bowl, then stir in the maple syrup, ginger, and cinnamon. Mix gently but thoroughly.

3. Meanwhile, in a large bowl, toss the diced apples with the coconut sugar, vanilla, cinnamon, and salt until the apples are coated. Spread the apples evenly on the prepared sheet pan. Dot the coconut oil evenly over the apples.

4. Transfer the apples to the oven with the sweet potatoes and bake for 10 minutes, stirring halfway through, until the apples are slightly soft and golden.

5. To make the toasts: Smear about 1 tablespoon of the sweet potato spread on each toast. Top with 2 tablespoons cinnamon apples. Drizzle almond butter over each toast and top with pumpkin seeds and shredded coconut. Drizzle with a touch of maple syrup and enjoy!

MAPLE CASHEW CREAM AND BANANA TOAST WITH SUPER SEED CRUNCH

MAKES 4 SERVINGS

This toast is simple but feels indulgent and luxurious with its layered textures and flavors. Perfect for any breakfast or brunch that you want to be just a little *extra* special.

MAPLE CASHEW CREAM

½ cup raw cashews
3 dates, pitted and soaked in hot water for 10 minutes
1 tablespoon pure maple syrup
½ tablespoon pure vanilla extract
Pinch of sea salt

SUPER SEED CRUNCH

1 tablespoon hemp hearts
1 tablespoon black sesame seeds
2 tablespoons chopped raw pistachios
½ teaspoon ground cinnamon

TOASTS

4 slices bread of your choice, toasted
1 large banana, thinly sliced
Pure maple syrup, for drizzling

1. To make the maple cashew cream: In a small high-powered blender, combine the cashews, drained dates, maple syrup, vanilla, 2 tablespoons water, and the sea salt and blend until smooth and creamy. If the mixture is too thick to blend, scrape the sides and add more water, 1 tablespoon at a time. Pour into a bowl and refrigerate until it's time to build the toasts!

2. To make the super seed crunch: In a small bowl, combine the hemp hearts, sesame seeds, pistachios, and cinnamon. Set aside.

3. To make the toasts: Spread about 1 tablespoon maple cashew cream on each slice of toast (refrigerate any leftover cream in a covered jar for up to 5 days). Top with banana slices and drizzle with maple syrup. Sprinkle the super seed crunch on top and serve. So easy and delicious!

ROASTED STREET CORN AVO TOAST

MAKES 4 SERVINGS

This combination of smoky sweet corn, creamy, tart avocado, and vegan cashew cheese is mind-blowing. Avocado lovers, rejoice!

ROASTED CORN

1 tablespoon vegan butter, melted
2 ears corn, husked
1 teaspoon annatto powder or paprika
1 teaspoon chipotle powder
Kosher salt
2 small cloves garlic, minced
1 teaspoon grated lime zest
½ jalapeño, seeded and finely minced
¼ cup chopped fresh cilantro

TOASTS

2 avocados, sliced
¼ teaspoon kosher salt
¼ teaspoon freshly ground black pepper
2 teaspoons fresh lime juice, plus lime wedges for squeezing
4 slices bread of your choice, toasted
4 tablespoons crumbled vegan cashew cheese (optional, but my favorite brand for this is Miyoko's)
Quick-Pickled Red Onions (optional; page 129)

1. Preheat the oven to 400°F. Line a baking sheet with foil.

2. To make the roasted corn: Rub melted butter over each ear of corn and sprinkle with annatto powder, chipotle powder, and salt to taste. Place the corn on the prepared pan and roast for 35 to 40 minutes, flipping halfway through, until golden yellow and toasted. Let rest for a few minutes to cool.

3. Lay the cobs flat on your cutting board and cut down one side at a time to remove the kernels. Place the kernels in a medium bowl and mix in the garlic, lime zest, jalapeño, and cilantro. Set aside.

4. Place the avocado slices on a plate and sprinkle with the salt, pepper, and lime juice.

5. Evenly divide the avocado slices among the toasts and top each with heaping tablespoons of roasted corn, crumbled vegan cheese (if using), and pickled red onion (if using). Top with a little squeeze of lime. Enjoy this ridiculously fabulous avo toast like the ridiculously fabulous human you are!

MAKE-IT-YOUR-OWN (MIYO) SMOOTHIES + SMOOTHIE BOWL GUIDE

Dealing with blenders and so many different milks, greens, superfoods, and spices can easily become overwhelming. But a go-to formula significantly helps with making smoothies and smoothie bowls that are hassle-free, taste good, are unique, and are packed with tons of nutrition and flavor. Try my favorite smoothie and smoothie bowl recipes starting on page 176, or use the MIYO Smoothies and Smoothie Bowls guide on pages 174–75 to get creative and comfortable with making tasty and nourishing smoothies on your own!

If your smoothie is too thin, add these thickening ingredients:

* Plant protein powder
* Chia seeds
* Flaxseed meal
* More ice
* More frozen banana
* Peeled and pitted avocado

If your smoothie is too thick, loosen with more liquid. Adding more liquid will most likely dilute the other flavors in your smoothie, so be sure to taste and adjust as you go!

Smoothies

MAKES 1 OR 2 SERVINGS

LIQUID

½ to 1+ cups

Any plant milk (some of my favorites are oat, cashew, coconut, and almond!)

Coconut water or plain water (I rarely use plain water because it doesn't add flavor)

FRUIT

½ to 2 cups, fresh or frozen

KEY: Bananas! It's essential to use fresh or frozen bananas as the base for most smoothies. It adds creaminess and natural sweetness. I usually use 1 medium or large banana for my smoothies or smoothie bowls.

Seasonal fruit of any kind (see chart on page 130 for a list)

Berries always work!

VEG

½ to 1 cup, fresh or frozen

Spinach
Kale
Swiss chard
Collard greens
Try lettuce sometime for a refreshing addition!
Steamed frozen zucchini
Steamed frozen cauliflower

NOURISHING FATS

½ to 2 tablespoons

Nut or seed butters
Chia seeds
Hemp hearts
Flaxseed meal

POWER PLUS OPTIONS (SEE PAGE 128)

"FANCY" THINGS

Purees (like butternut or pumpkin)

Plant-based yogurts (if using, replace up to half of your liquid!)

Plant protein powders

Syrups (pure maple, agave)

Spices (ground cinnamon, ground ginger)

Rolled oats (1 to 2 tablespoons; gluten-free if needed)

Cocoa powder (up to 1 tablespoon)

ICE ICE BABY

You may or may not want the extra coldness of ice, but if you do, use about ½ cup!

Smoothie Bowls

MAKES 1 OR 2 SERVINGS

Smoothie bowls are basically smoothies blessed with extra thickness and infinite toppings. They're one of my favorite things to make when I want something a little more substantial and filling than a smoothie, but still packed with lots of nutrients and flavor.

To make smoothie bowls, make the following tweaks to the amounts in the smoothie chart (page 174)!

* Reduce the amount of liquid to ¼ to ⅔ cup. You can use yogurt instead of liquid, or a combination of both.
* Use frozen bananas only
* The bowl should include at least ½ cup frozen ingredients in addition to the banana
* Limit the amount of fresh produce—try to use only frozen fruit and veg if possible
* Toppings are the best part of smoothie bowls, IMO. Try having some fun with the ingredients and flavors you layer on top of your bowl. Ideas to try:

Granola	**Nut or seed butter**
Shredded coconut or coconut flakes	**Chia seeds**
Nuts	**Hemp hearts**
Fruit of your choice (orange slices are surprisingly fantastic on top of some smoothie bowls!)	**Pumpkin seeds**
	Sunflower seeds
	Flaxseed meal
	Any superfood!

If your bowl isn't blending (this can be tricky based on the power of the blender), stop and stir the mixture/scrape down the sides or add a touch more liquid to help it blend.

You can experiment with new and different combos, or get inspired by some of my favorites in the pages to come!

FOREST FUEL GREEN SMOOTHIE

MAKES 1 OR 2 SERVINGS

A green smoothie that is hydrating, refreshing, perfectly sweet, and most important, *doesn't taste like grass. No grass-tasting smoothies allowed!*

1 medium banana
½ cup spinach
1 cup frozen pineapple chunks
1 scoop your favorite vanilla plant protein powder (I like Garden of Life powders!)
½ cup unsweetened coconut water
½ cup unsweetened oat milk
Power Plus: Add 1 teaspoon matcha powder to stay focused and calm!
½ cup ice (optional)

Blend all the ingredients until smooth!

BODY BENEFITS: *Protein, fiber, iron, calcium, natural electrolytes*

BLUEBERRY-COCOA-GINGER SMOOTHIE

MAKES 1 OR 2 SERVINGS

This fruity, chocolaty, nutty, and spicy (depending on how much you crank up the ginger) smoothie with a sturdy base of healthy fats, fiber, and low-glycemic fruits will give you lasting energy. Plus, any way to start or push through the day is always made better with chocolate. :)

1 frozen banana
1 cup frozen blueberries
1 tablespoon nut or seed butter (I love almond and cashew!)
1 tablespoon hemp hearts
2 teaspoons unsweetened cocoa powder
2 tablespoons rolled oats (gluten-free if needed)
½ to 1 tablespoon grated fresh ginger, to taste
1 cup unsweetened oat milk
½ cup ice (optional)

Blend all the ingredients until smooth!

BODY BENEFITS: *Lowers cholesterol, high in antioxidants, aids in muscle repair, good fats, heart healthy*

COZY APPLE BUTTERNUT SHAKE

MAKES 1 OR 2 SERVINGS

I love the flavors of fall and often crave them through spring and summer. This smoothie is perfect to enjoy during the transition from fall/winter to spring, or year-round if like me your food mood is #fallforever. Plus, I love a good shake that keeps me full and energized as a hearty breakfast or snack!

1 frozen banana
½ cup steamed frozen cauliflower florets
½ cup diced apple (Red Delicious is always a go-to!)
½ cup coconut-milk yogurt
½ cup unsweetened oat milk
⅔ cup canned butternut squash puree
½ to 1 teaspoon ground cinnamon, to taste
½ teaspoon ground ginger
Pinch of ground cardamom
Power Plus: Add 1 teaspoon maca powder to boost mood, brain, and energy!

Blend all the ingredients until smooth!

BODY BENEFITS *Antioxidants, bone-healthy vitamins, immunity boost, skin protection, fiber*

PB&J SMOOTHIE BOWL

MAKES 1 OR 2 SERVINGS

A traditional childhood favorite transformed into a creamy, nutty, and tart smoothie bowl! PB&J is officially *alll* the way glowed up with a trio of frozen berries, some spices that pop, and out-of-this-world toppings!

1 frozen banana
1 cup frozen strawberries
¼ cup frozen blueberries
¼ cup frozen raspberries
¼ cup coconut-milk yogurt
2 tablespoons nut butter of your choice
2 tablespoons jam of your choice
½ tablespoon grated fresh ginger (optional)
1 teaspoon ground cinnamon
Power Plus: Add 1½ teaspoons flaxseed meal to get in your essential omega-3s!

OPTIONAL (BUT HIGHLY RECOMMENDED) TOPPINGS
Berry jam
Granola (see page 158)
Fresh berries
Nut or seed butter
Roasted peanuts

Blend all the ingredients in a high-powered blender (see Tip) until thick, smooth, and creamy! Depending on your blender, you may have to stop, stir the mixture, scrape down the sides, and/or add a touch more liquid to help it blend. Pour the mixture into one or two bowls. If desired, top with jam, granola, berries, nut butter, or nuts. Enjoy this cool, creamy, nutty goodness!

Tip: Why a high-powered blender? Blending frozen ingredients with small amounts of liquid can sometimes present a challenge for regular blenders to incorporate everything smoothly. Adding more liquid always helps, but this will loosen your smoothie bowl.

TROPICAL CITRUS SMOOTHIE BOWL

MAKES 1 OR 2 SERVINGS

The blank canvas of high-fiber and potassium-rich zucchini helps it blend well with powerhouse tropical and citrusy flavors. Refreshingly sweet pineapple and rich mango combine classically while a little orange zest brings everything to life. Toss in some small-but-mighty chia seeds for added protein, fiber, and omega-3s!

1 frozen banana
½ cup frozen zucchini chunks
½ cup frozen pineapple chunks
1 cup frozen mango
¼ cup oat milk
1 teaspoon orange zest
½ teaspoon ground cinnamon
Power Plus: Add 1 to 2 teaspoons chia seeds for a protein and fiber boost!

OPTIONAL (BUT HIGHLY RECOMMENDED) TOPPINGS
Strawberries
Banana
Mango
Kiwi
Coconut flakes or shredded cocconut
Granola (see page 158)

Blend all the ingredients in a high-powered blender until thick, smooth, and creamy! Depending on your blender, you may have to stop, stir the mixture, scrape down the sides, and/or add a touch more liquid to help it blend. Pour the mixture into one or two bowls. If desired, top with strawberries, banana, mango, kiwi, coconut, and granola. Enjoy this bowl—it's bound to bring some sunshine to your day!

PINK POWER SMOOTHIE BOWL

MAKES 1 OR 2 SERVINGS

A traditional combination of ingredients makes for a refreshing bowl that can really be built out any way you'd like! I enjoy this recipe because it lets the toppings shine, and the simple base makes them interchangeable. This bowl is just waiting for you to experiment with tropical, traditional, chocolaty, and superfood toppings.

1 frozen banana
¼ cup frozen raspberries
¼ cup frozen strawberries
⅔ cup coconut milk
1 tablespoon pure maple syrup
Power Plus: 2 tablespoons dried goji berries

OPTIONAL (BUT HIGHLY RECOMMENDED) TOPPINGS
Seasonal fruits (see chart on page 130 for ideas)
Nut or seed butter
Melted vegan chocolate
Raw nuts or seeds
Granola (see page 158)

Blend all the ingredients in a high-powered blender until thick, smooth, and creamy! Depending on your blender, you may have to stop, stir the mixture, scrape down the sides, and/or add a touch more liquid to help it blend. Pour the mixture into one or two bowls. If desired, add toppings. Enjoy!

BUILD-A-BOWL WORKSHOP

Plates are out and bowls are in—but putting together the elements of a bowl can become daunting, with all the veggies, proteins, toppings, and dressings to choose from. Knowing where and how to layer for maximum nourishment *and* flavor is an art that I'm really excited to help you master. Use the guide below to start making bowls like a boss—and use the recipes starting on page 186 as inspiration for taking your bowls to the next level!

Keys to a Fire Bowl

MAKES 1 OR 2 SERVINGS

GREEN BASE (OPTIONAL)	**Up to 3 cups to boost nutrition**	Kale Arugula Beet greens Spinach Spring greens Romaine lettuce Sprouts Microgreens Swiss chard
CARBS/GRAINS	**Up to 2 cups**	Rice Quinoa Potatoes of any kind Squash Plantains Millet Pasta Couscous

PROTEINS	**Up to 16 ounces**	Tofu
		Tempeh
		Edamame
		Chickpeas
		Lentils
VEG	**¼ to 2 cups each; pick 2 or 3 or combine as you'd like! Roast, sauté, or use them raw.**	Cucumbers
		Bell peppers
		Cauliflower
		Tomatoes (I know, it's a fruit, but it chills with the veg)
		Radishes
		Mushrooms
		Red onion (raw or pickled)
		Broccoli
		Green beans
		Shredded cabbage
		Avocado
FRUIT (OPTIONAL)	**¼ to 1½ cups; make sure your choice complements the other elements of the bowl**	Pineapple
		Apples
		Strawberries
		Blueberries
		Dried fruit (like cranberries)
DRESSINGS	**⅓ to 1 cup**	Head to page 234 for some killer dressings and sauces to try!
FUN STUFF		Fresh herbs: basil, mint, cilantro, parsley, thyme
		Nuts
		Seeds
		Buffalo wings sauce
		Scotch bonnet sauce
		Chili paste
		Tahini
		Jalapeño slices

TEMPEH AND KALE BOWL WITH CILANTRO-TAHINI DRESSING

MAKES 4 SERVINGS

Since I grew up in Arizona, there is a big place in my heart for Southwestern flavors. I love using the smoky and toasty undertones of spices like cumin and paprika to elevate my proteins and add a pop to dressings. This bowl is hearty and layered with freshness and flavor. Every time I eat it, I swear I can feel my cells doing a little happy dance.

KALE
2 bunches de-stemmed kale, chopped, or one 5-ounce bag baby kale
1 tablespoon fresh lemon juice
1 tablespoon olive oil

TEMPEH
Two 8-ounce packages tempeh
2 tablespoons fresh lime juice
1 teaspoon tamari
½ tablespoon garlic powder
2 teaspoons ground cumin
2 teaspoons dried oregano
1 teaspoon paprika

Kosher salt
1 tablespoon olive oil

BOWL COMPONENTS
Kernels cut from 4 medium ears corn
1 to 2 cups sliced grape tomatoes, to taste
½ red onion, thinly sliced
Cilantro-Tahini Dressing (page 235)

OPTIONAL (BUT HIGHLY RECOMMENDED) TOPPINGS
Sliced or diced avocado
Cooked black beans, chilled
Raw pumpkin seeds

1. To make the kale: In a large bowl, massage the lemon juice and olive oil into the chopped kale (see Tip on page 187) for 2 to 3 minutes. Cover and place in the fridge until it's time to build your bowl.

2. To make the tempeh: Crumble the tempeh into a large bowl. Add the lime juice, tamari, garlic powder, cumin, oregano, paprika, and salt to taste and stir until the tempeh is fully coated.

3. In a large skillet, heat the olive oil over medium heat. When the pan is hot, add the tempeh. Sauté for 5 to 8 minutes, until golden brown and slightly crispy. Remove from the heat and set aside.

4. To assemble the bowls: In a large bowl, combine the corn kernels, tomatoes, and onion. Place a handful of kale in each of four bowls and top with the corn mix. Add the tempeh crumbles, a drizzle of the dressing, and any optional topping you're including. Enjoy this bowl of Southwestern nourishment!

Tip: BTW! Massaging kale helps to break down and soften its rough texture, making it easier to eat.

CARROT-CHICKPEA-QUINOA BOWL WITH MAPLE HARISSA DRESSING

MAKES 4 SERVINGS

A really approachable bowl with sweet, savory, and smoky flavors in harmony. It's grown-up and simple all at the same time!

ROASTED CHIPOTLE CHICKPEAS

One 15-ounce can chickpeas, drained and rinsed
1 tablespoon olive oil
Kosher salt
1 tablespoon garlic powder
½ tablespoon paprika
1 teaspoon ground cumin
1 teaspoon ground turmeric
½ teaspoon chipotle powder

SALAD

1 bunch baby kale
2 cups baby arugula
2 cups peeled and shredded carrots
½ cup chopped fresh parsley
1 tablespoon olive oil
2 cups cooked quinoa (cooked according to package instructions)
1 small red onion, thinly sliced
¼ cup raw sunflower seeds
3 tablespoons Maple Harissa Dressing (page 236), plus more for serving

1. To make the chickpeas: Preheat the oven to 400°F. Line a sheet pan with parchment paper.

2. Pat the chickpeas dry with a paper towel or kitchen towel and place them on the prepared sheet pan. Toss them with the olive oil and salt to taste. Spread them evenly on the sheet pan and roast for 20 to 25 minutes, until crispy.

3. Transfer the chickpeas to a bowl and immediately toss them with the garlic powder, paprika, cumin, turmeric, and chipotle powder. Set aside.

4. To make the salad: In a large bowl, toss the kale, arugula, carrots, and parsley. Drizzle with the olive oil and use your hands to massage the vegetables for about 30 seconds to 1 minute.

5. Mix in the cooked quinoa, red onion, sunflower seeds, and the dressing.

6. Divide the salad among four bowls and top each with chickpeas. Drizzle the bowls with extra dressing and enjoy! *Eat with your pinky up for the ultimate bougie bowl experience.*

CREAMY BEET SPAGHETTI WITH GARLICKY GREENS

MAKES 4 SERVINGS

I've never been the biggest fan of beets, but knowing just how incredible they are for our health (they're heart-healthy and immunity boosting and improve digestion), I knew I had to find a way to transform them into something I could truly enjoy. Whipping roasted beets into a garlicky, nutty, and sweet sauce completely flipped my view of them, making them sophisticated and multidimensional. Plus, eating pink pasta is honestly the most adorable thing ever.

BEET SAUCE AND PASTA

2 large red beets, greens attached
½ cup olive oil, plus more for drizzling
Kosher salt
1 pound gluten-free spaghetti
4 garlic cloves, peeled
½ cup raw slivered almonds
2 tablespoons red wine vinegar
1 tablespoon dried oregano
1 tablespoon dried parsley

MUSHROOMS AND GREENS

1 tablespoon coconut oil
2½ heaping cups sliced shiitake mushroom caps (about 8.6 ounces untrimmed)
1 cup sliced spinach
1 teaspoon kosher salt
2 teaspoons dried oregano
1 teaspoon garlic powder
¼ teaspoon freshly ground black pepper
Pine nuts (optional)

1. Preheat the oven to 400°F.

2. Cut the beet tops off and slice 1 cup of the greens for this recipe and reserve the rest for another delicious use. Peel the beets and roughly cut them into chunks. Place them on a sheet pan and drizzle with enough olive oil to lightly coat them. Roast for 35 to 40 minutes, turning halfway through with a spatula, until the beets are tender.

3. Meanwhile, bring a large pot of salted water to a boil. Add the pasta and cook until al dente.

4. In a food processor, combine the garlic and almonds and pulse until the almonds are a fine meal and the garlic is minced. Add the roasted beets, ½ cup olive oil, vinegar, 1 teaspoon kosher salt, oregano, and parsley and pulse into a smooth sauce. Set aside.

5. To make the mushrooms and greens: In a medium skillet, heat the coconut oil over medium heat. Add the mushrooms and sauté until soft and juicy, about 5 minutes. Add the reserved sliced beet greens and the spinach and cook, stirring, for 2 to 3 minutes, ensuring the greens aren't fully wilted. Season with the salt, oregano, garlic powder, and pepper and mix to combine. Cover and set aside over low heat.

6. Toss the pasta in the beet sauce and top with greens and mushrooms. Sprinkle with pine nuts (if using). Serve hot.

NUTTY SUNFLOWER SPRING ROLL BOWL

MAKES 4 SERVINGS

Homemade veggie spring rolls are one of my favorite things to eat. But I don't make them too often because I cannot stand dealing with annoying and clumpy rice paper! This spring roll bowl is a solid solution to my frustration—it has all the flavors and ingredients I adore without the hassle!

BAKED SUNFLOWER CHILI TEMPEH

1 to 2 teaspoons red Thai chili paste, to taste

2 tablespoons toasted sesame oil

3 tablespoons fresh lime juice

¼ cup sunflower seed butter

¼ cup pure maple syrup

¼ cup tamari (or soy sauce or liquid aminos)

1 teaspoon kosher salt

Two 8-ounce packages tempeh, cut into 1-inch-thick slices

BOWL COMPONENTS

4 cups cooked pad Thai rice noodles (from 8 ounces uncooked)

¼ head red cabbage, thinly sliced

5 small carrots, peeled and sliced into thin rounds

4 mini cucumbers, sliced into thin rounds

2 large bell peppers, any color, sliced into thin strips

⅓ cup thinly sliced basil leaves

5-Spice Sunflower Sauce (page 238)

2 scallions, chopped

Raw sunflower seeds

1. To make the baked tempeh: In a large bowl, vigorously whisk the chili paste, sesame oil, lime juice, sunflower seed butter, maple syrup, tamari, and salt together. Add the tempeh slices and toss to combine, making sure all the slices are coated with the marinade. Cover the bowl and marinate in the refrigerator for 1½ to 2 hours.

2. Preheat the oven to 375°F. Line a sheet pan with parchment paper.

3. Place the marinated tempeh slices along with the remaining marinade on the prepared sheet pan and bake for 25 to 30 minutes, until the tempeh is golden and the marinade is soaked in.

4. To build the bowls: Divide the noodles, veggies, tempeh, basil, sunflower sauce, scallions, and sunflower seeds among four bowls. Enjoy!

ISLANDER LIVELY BOWL

MAKES 4 SERVINGS

Both of my parents are from the Caribbean, so I've grown up appreciating the magic that happens when sweet and savory ingredients come together. The combination of smoky mushrooms, sweet pineapple salsa, coconut undertones, and supporting acidic and savory pops of flavor is what makes this bowl so divine. And don't you dare skip out on the cilantro aioli—it is cooling, creamy, and simply the real deal.

PINEAPPLE SALSA

1½ cups small-diced fresh pineapple
½ cup chopped fresh cilantro
½ cup small-diced red onion
¾ cup diced cherry tomatoes
1 jalapeño, seeded and minced
2 teaspoons fresh lime juice
Kosher salt and freshly ground black pepper

SHIITAKE MUSHROOMS

½ cup tamari
¼ cup toasted sesame oil
¼ cup pure maple syrup

2 tablespoons sriracha
5 cups sliced shiitake mushroom caps (about 13 ounces)
1 tablespoon coconut oil

BOWL COMPONENTS

2 to 4 cups cooked brown rice (cooked according to package instructions)
Cilantro Aioli (page 237)
1 medium avocado, sliced
Grilled pineapple
Quick-Pickled Red Onions (page 129)

1. To make the pineapple salsa: In a medium bowl, combine the pineapple, cilantro, onion, tomatoes, jalapeño, and lime juice, and toss to mix. Season with salt and black pepper to taste. Cover and refrigerate until needed.

2. To make the shiitake mushrooms: In a large bowl, whisk together the tamari, sesame oil, maple syrup, and sriracha. Add the mushrooms and toss to combine, making sure all mushrooms are coated with marinade. Cover the bowl and marinate in the refrigerator for at least 20 minutes.

3. Drain the marinade liquid from the mushrooms. In a large skillet, heat the coconut oil over medium heat. Add the mushrooms and sear on one side without stirring for 2 to 3 minutes, until crispy. Flip the mushrooms with a spatula and cook for 3 to 5 minutes, until the mushrooms are crisp on both sides.

4. To serve: In each of four bowls, place ½ to 1 cup brown rice, one-quarter of the mushrooms, and a scoop of pineapple salsa, with a dollop of cilantro aioli on top. Placed sliced avocado, grilled pineapples, and pickled onions on each bowl as well. Enjoy the harmonious smoky savory sweetness of this bowl!

Soulful
Staples

OVEN-FRIED MUSHROOMS

MAKES 4 SERVINGS

No matter how healthfully we eat, there's no denying that crispy food is heavenly, and I'm definitely not about to pretend it's not! This recipe satisfies both my love of mushrooms and my crispiness cravings, but uses a little bit healthier frying technique. It's a great sub for traditional fried proteins and can be paired with sweet and savory foods . . . check it out with French Toast on page 146!

DRY MIX

½ cup brown rice flour
½ cup regular or gluten-free panko bread crumbs
½ tablespoon nutritional yeast
2 teaspoons sea salt
1 teaspoon garlic powder
1 teaspoon onion powder
1 teaspoon paprika
½ teaspoon ground turmeric
½ teaspoon freshly ground black pepper
¼ teaspoon baking powder

WET MIX

½ cup unsweetened oat milk
½ tablespoon fresh lemon juice
1 tablespoon Buffalo wings sauce (see Tip on page 198)

MUSHROOMS

Two 9-ounce maitake mushrooms, each cut into 4 or 5 thick slices, any dirt/residue brushed off
4 tablespoons vegan butter, melted

1. Preheat the oven to 425°F.

2. To make the dry mix: In a medium bowl, combine all the ingredients. Set aside.

3. To make the wet mix: In a medium bowl, whisk the oat milk and lemon juice to combine. Set aside for 10 minutes, until curdled. Add the Buffalo sauce to the milk mixture and whisk to incorporate. Set the milk mixture aside.

4. Place a 9 × 13-inch metal baking pan (not glass) in the oven to preheat for 5 to 10 minutes.

5. Meanwhile, to prepare the mushrooms: Dip a mushroom slice into the milk mixture, coating thoroughly. Shake off any excess liquid, then drop the mushroom slice into the seasoned flour mixture, tossing to coat all sides. Place the mushroom on a plate and set aside while you coat the rest of the pieces.

6. Remove the hot baking pan from the oven and pour the melted butter in the pan to coat it thoroughly. Arrange the mushroom pieces on the butter, with space between the pieces on all sides so that the mushrooms fry.

7. Roast for 12 minutes, then flip the mushroom pieces over and roast for 12 minutes more, until golden brown and crisp.

8. Rest for 5 minutes before serving.

Tip: I keep it classic and use Frank's RedHot Buffalo WIngs Sauce—which is vegan, by the way! Be sure to do your research on other brands, as they may contain butter.

STRAIGHT FIRE MAC AND CHEESE

MAKES 2 TO 4 SERVINGS

This mac and cheese is straight fire—hence the name. Zero dairy, but 100 percent rich, smoky cheesiness. I literally melt in my chair every time I get to dig into this timeless, comforting meal. It's mind-blowingly easy and delicious!

MAC SAUCE

1 medium carrot, peeled
½ cup raw cashews, soaked in hot water for at least 10 minutes
½ cup canned or home-cooked cannellini beans, drained
½ cup nutritional yeast
½ cup vegetable broth
1 tablespoon vegan butter

1 teaspoon garlic powder
1 teaspoon onion powder
¼ to ½ teaspoon chipotle powder
Kosher salt

NOODLES AND CHEESE

16 ounces gluten-free elbow macaroni
1 cup shredded vegan cheese of your choice (optional)

1. To make the mac sauce: Place the carrot in a steamer basket (or a sieve or colander). Fill a wide saucepan (that can fit the steamer) with about 1 inch of water and bring to a simmer over medium-high heat. Cook the carrot in the steamer over the simmering water for 5 to 10 minutes, until the carrot is tender.

2. Transfer the carrot to a blender or food processor. Add the cashews, beans, nutritional yeast, broth, butter, garlic powder, onion powder, chipotle powder, and salt to taste and blend until smooth.

3. To make the noodles and cheese: In a large pot of boiling salted water, cook the macaroni to al dente. Drain and transfer to a bowl. Pour the mac sauce and shredded vegan cheese over the hot, freshly cooked pasta and stir, ensuring all the pasta is covered with sauce. The hot pasta will heat the sauce.

4. Enjoy and get ready to want more! :)

SAVE MONEY (AND TBH, BE LESS GASSY): MAKE YOUR BEANS FROM SCRATCH!

MAKES ABOUT 2½ CUPS COOKED BEANS FOR EVERY 1 CUP DRIED BEANS

This process requires more patience than canned beans, but it's easy if you plan ahead a little. Not only is it super inexpensive to use dried beans, but it's especially helpful if you struggle with indigestion or gas when eating beans. If you think you may be too busy to make this work, try starting the process on a Friday or Saturday night. The most time is spent soaking the beans, which doesn't require much attention—you'll spend 2 hours or less cooking them! The longer the soak time, the faster the beans cook, the better the texture, and the more the beans break down the complex sugars that cause gas.

1. In a colander, rinse the dried beans. Place the beans in a large pot. For every 1 cup beans, add 4 cups water. Let the beans soak at room temperature for at least 8 or refrigerated for up to 24 hours.

2. Drain the beans in a colander and rinse well with cold water.

3. Return the beans to the pot and add 5 cups water for every original cup of beans. Set the pot over medium-high heat and bring to a boil. Give the beans a stir, turn off the heat, and cover the pot. Let it sit for at least 2 and for up to 8 hours. Drain the beans once more and rinse super well with cold water to remove all the soaking liquid. This helps to reduce the gas effects.

4. Return the beans to the pot and add enough water to cover them by 2 to 3 inches. Bring to a simmer over medium-high heat, reduce the heat to a simmer, and cook for 45 minutes to 2 hours. Periodically check the beans for your desired doneness (softness), adding more water as needed so that the beans don't dry out as they cook.

5. Drain and use as needed, plain or lightly seasoned, as you wish. To store, place the beans in a sealed container and store in the fridge for up to 5 days. To freeze, allow to cool completely and store in a freezer-friendly container.

SWEET PEA AND CORN RISOTTO

MAKES 4 SERVINGS

When I visited Italy for the first time, I was fascinated by all of the risotto varia-tions I got to try. My favorite was asparagus and sweet pea! While nothing can compare to authentic food straight from an Italian kitchen, I was inspired to get back home and experiment with making this irresistibly rich and creamy risotto with hints of savory-sweetness.

MIX-INS

Salt

2 cups frozen green peas, 1 cup left frozen, 1 cup thawed

2 ears corn, husked

RISOTTO

5 cups vegetable broth

1 tablespoon olive oil

1 tablespoon vegan butter, plus 2 tablespoons (optional), for serving

½ medium yellow onion, cut into medium dice

4 garlic cloves, minced

Kosher salt

2 cups Arborio rice

Freshly ground black pepper

2 teaspoons garlic powder

½ to 1 cup shredded vegan cheese (I recommend parmesan or mozzarella), to taste

TOPPINGS

¾ teaspoon fresh lemon juice

1½ teaspoons extra virgin olive oil

Kosher salt

Freshly ground black pepper

Handful of microgreens

¼ cup roughly chopped fresh parsley

Grated lemon zest

1. To prepare the mix-ins: Set up a bowl of ice and water. In a saucepan of boiling salted water, blanch the 1 cup frozen peas for 1 minute. Drain the peas and shock them in the ice water. When the peas have cooled, drain them and pat them dry with paper towels. Transfer to a food processor and puree until smooth, scraping down the sides as needed. Set aside.

2. Grate 1 ear of the corn using the large holes of a box grater. Place the corn pulp in a bowl. Slice the kernels from the remaining ear of corn by laying it flat on your cutting board and slicing down one side at a time. Add the kernels to the corn pulp and set aside.

3. To make the risotto: In a medium saucepan, heat the broth over low heat until lightly simmering.

4. In a deep saucepan, heat the olive oil and 1 tablespoon butter over medium-high heat. Add the onion and garlic and sauté for 3 to 5 minutes, until translucent. Sprinkle with a pinch of salt. Add the rice and stir over low heat until it begins to whiten.

5. Add ½ cup of the broth and salt and pepper to taste and simmer over low heat, stirring frequently until almost all of the liquid has evaporated. Add 1½ cups of the broth and simmer, stirring frequently, until the liquid is almost fully absorbed. Add the rest of the broth ½ cup at a time, stirring frequently and waiting until each ½ cup is absorbed before adding more. This process will take 20 to 25 minutes, until the rice is cooked and creamy.

6. When the rice is nearly done, mix in the garlic powder, vegan cheese, pea puree, thawed peas, and corn mixture. Adjust the seasoning as desired and remove from the heat. Stir in the additional 2 tablespoons vegan butter (if using).

7. To prepare the toppings: In a small bowl, combine the lemon juice, olive oil, and salt and pepper to taste. Drizzle the dressing onto the microgreens and toss to coat.

8. Divide the risotto among four bowls and top each with microgreens, parsley, and lemon zest. Enjoy immediately!

RED-HOT ROASTED CAULIFLOWER STEAKS WITH CHIMICHURRI SAUCE

MAKES 4 SERVINGS

Knowing how to season and roast a good cauliflower steak is essential in my house, so I'm passing this favorite recipe of mine on to you! Because of cauliflower's neutral flavor, it's a great canvas for spices and sauces that really pop. Serve with your favorite veggies and grains!

ROASTED CAULIFLOWER

1 tablespoon garlic powder
1 tablespoon paprika
1 tablespoon dried thyme
Dash of cayenne pepper
Kosher salt
1 medium head cauliflower, cut through the core into about four ½-inch-thick slices
2 tablespoons olive oil

CHIMICHURRI SAUCE

½ cup fresh cilantro, leaves and stems
½ cup fresh parsley, leaves and stems
¼ cup fresh basil leaves
4 garlic cloves, peeled
¼ cup olive oil
¼ cup white wine vinegar
Kosher salt

1. To roast the cauliflower: Preheat the oven to 425°F. Line a sheet pan with parchment paper.

2. In a medium bowl, combine the garlic powder, paprika, thyme, cayenne, and salt to taste.

3. Arrange the cauliflower "steaks" on the prepared sheet pan and drizzle them with 1 tablespoon of the olive oil. Evenly sprinkle the herb/spice mixture over both sides of each cauliflower steak. Drizzle the cauliflower steaks with the remaining 1 tablespoon olive oil.

4. Roast for 20 to 25 minutes, until the cauliflower is golden and crisp on top.

5. Meanwhile, to make the chimichurri sauce: In a food processor, combine the cilantro, parsley, basil, garlic, olive oil, vinegar, and salt to taste and blend until smooth. Set aside.

6. Drizzle the steaks with chimichurri sauce and serve.

MY MAMA'S JAMAICAN RICE AND PEAS WITH CURRY MUSHROOMS

MAKES 4 TO 6 SERVINGS

My mom learned how to make authentic Jamaican rice and peas from my great-grandma, and we often joke that she never could have imagined this shortcut version—no grating coconut or boiling peas for hours required. This version may take a quick 15 to 25 minutes to make, but does *not* skimp on the beloved flavor.

RICE AND PEAS

One 13.5-ounce can full-fat coconut milk
3 cups brown rice
Two 15.5-ounce cans red kidney beans, drained and rinsed
½ cup fresh thyme leaves
4 scallions, smashed and roughly chopped
1 tablespoon allspice berries
2 tablespoons garlic powder
2 tablespoons onion powder
1 large Scotch bonnet pepper (see Tip on page 210; pierce the pepper to release flavor while cooking)
Kosher salt

CURRY MUSHROOMS

2 tablespoons coconut oil
4 large garlic cloves, minced
1 large yellow onion, roughly chopped
2 medium Yukon Gold potatoes, cut into ¾-inch chunks
3 tablespoons fresh thyme
4 large portobello mushrooms, cut into 1-inch slices
14 medium to large shiitake mushrooms, stems discarded, caps cut into ¾-inch slices
2 tablespoons Jamaican curry powder
1 tablespoon paprika
1 teaspoon ground allspice
Kosher salt
3 cups mushroom or vegetable broth
3 large bell peppers (yellow, red, green), thinly sliced
1 cup full-fat coconut milk
4 large scallions, thinly sliced
1 cup chopped fresh cilantro
½ to 1 tablespoon Scotch bonnet pepper sauce (optional; my mom always uses the Grace brand!), to taste

1. To make the rice and peas: In a deep saucepan, combine the rice, coconut milk, 2 cups water (see Tip on page 210), beans, thyme, scallions, allspice, garlic powder, onion powder, Scotch bonnet pepper, and salt to taste. Stir to combine and bring to a boil over high heat. Reduce the heat, cover, and cook for the amount of time listed on the brown rice package directions, until the rice is done. Remove from the heat, fluff the rice, and cover to retain the heat.

2. To make the curry mushrooms: In a large skillet, heat coconut oil over medium heat. Add the garlic and onion and cook for 2 minutes, stirring occasionally. Add the potatoes, thyme, mushrooms, curry powder, paprika, allspice, and salt to taste and stir to combine. Cover and cook for 5 minutes. Add the broth and simmer on medium-low heat for 15 minutes or until the potatoes are tender.

3. Add the bell peppers and coconut milk, cover, and simmer for 5 minutes. Stir in the scallions, cilantro, and Scotch bonnet sauce (if using).

4. Serve the curry mushrooms on top of a scoop of rice and peas.

Tip on Scotch bonnet peppers: This tip you're gonna love me for. From experience, I advise you to be very careful when using Scotch bonnet peppers. This pepper and its seeds pack a punch in the heat department, so do not touch your eyes or anything on your face while handling them or you will be very uncomfortably on fire. The amount of times I've had to flush my burning eyes after being reckless with the pepper is embarrassing! If you want to be super cautious, wear gloves!

Tip on rice: Depending on the brand of rice you use, the rice-to-liquid ratio and cooking times may vary. Please adjust accordingly.

POTACHOS (POTATO NACHOS) WITH GREEN CHILE CHEESE SAUCE

MAKES 4 TO 6 SERVINGS

Crispy baked potatoes, cheesy and spicy sauce, fresh and creamy avocado . . . what more could you ask for, and what more do I need to say? Bonus: This incredible green chile cheese sauce, a version of the mac sauce in the recipe on page 201, is terrific on its own as a dip with roasted potatoes or on tacos.

Olive oil
12 small to medium russet potatoes
Kosher salt and freshly ground black pepper

GREEN CHILE CHEESE SAUCE

1 medium carrot, peeled
½ cup raw cashews, soaked in hot water for 10 minutes
½ cup canned or cooked cannellini beans, drained
1 to 2 tablespoons canned chopped green chiles
½ cup nutritional yeast
½ cup vegetable broth
1 tablespoon vegan butter

1 to 2 teaspoons ground cumin, to taste
1 teaspoon garlic powder
1 teaspoon onion powder
Kosher salt

TOPPINGS

Shredded vegan mozzarella
2 or 3 avocados, diced
½ red onion, finely diced
1 cup quartered cherry tomatoes
2 jalapeños, seeded and finely diced
Chopped fresh cilantro
Any additional seasonal veggies you'd like (see chart on page 130 for ideas)

1. Preheat the oven to 425°F. Lightly oil a baking sheet pan with olive oil.

2. Fill a large pot with water and bring to a boil over high heat. Add the potatoes and boil for 20 minutes, until they are just cooked and can be easily pierced with a fork but are not yet soft and mushy.

3. Drain the water, pat the potatoes dry, and place them on the prepared pan. Using a fork or potato masher, lightly press down on each potato to smash it. Lightly brush the tops with olive oil and sprinkle with salt and pepper to taste.

4. Bake for 30 minutes, until the potatoes have a nice, crisp, golden top.

5. Meanwhile, to make the green chile cheese sauce: Place the carrot in a steamer basket (or a sieve or colander). Fill a wide saucepan (that can fit the steamer) with about 1 inch of water and bring to a simmer over medium-high heat. Cook the carrot in the steamer over the simmering water for 5 to 10 minutes, until the carrot is tender.

6. Cut in four and transfer the carrot to a blender or food processor and add the cashews, beans, green chiles, nutritional yeast, broth, butter, cumin, garlic powder, onion powder, and salt to taste and blend until smooth. Transfer to a small saucepan and heat.

7. Carefully remove the potatoes from the oven, sprinkle vegan mozzarella on top, and pop back into the oven for 3 to 5 minutes, until the cheese is melted.

8. Top with the diced avocados, red onion, cherry tomatoes, jalapeños, cilantro, sauce, and any additional vegetables. Enjoy this fun and messy meal that's perfect for sharing!

CRUNCHY MUSHROOM GRILLED CHEESE WITH GREEN QUEEN SAUCE

MAKES 4 SERVINGS

In my former days as a legitimate cheese addict, just plain grilled cheese (with like ten slices of cheddar) was one of my all-time favorites. This recipe is a major glow-up with gorgeous seared mushrooms and a lovely, herby Green Queen Dipping Sauce. It's elevated, but still the messy, crunchy, gooey sandwich we all know and love!

1½ tablespoons olive oil
4 medium maitake mushrooms (about 18 ounces total), cut into ½-inch-thick slices
½ tablespoon chipotle powder
1 tablespoon garlic powder
Sea salt

4 to 8 slices of your favorite vegan cheese, to taste
8 slices of your favorite bread
2 tablespoons vegan butter
Green Queen Dipping Sauce (page 238)

1. In a large skillet, heat ½ tablespoon of the olive oil over medium-high heat. Add the mushroom slices and sear for 3 minutes on one side. Drizzle 1 tablespoon of the olive oil over the mushrooms and sprinkle them with the chipotle powder, garlic powder, and salt to taste. Reduce the heat to medium, flip and cook for another 5 minutes on the second side.

2. Build your grilled cheeses by layering 1 or 2 slices of vegan cheese on each of 4 slices of bread. Top with the mushroom slices and the other slices of bread.

3. Heat the skillet used for the mushrooms over medium-high heat and melt 1 tablespoon of the vegan butter. Place two assembled sandwiches in the skillet and cook for 1 minute uncovered and 1 minute covered. Flip the sandwiches and repeat, cooking 1 minute uncovered and 1 minute covered. You want the vegan cheese to be nice and melted and the bread to be crisp. Repeat to make the other two sandwiches.

4. Enjoy your grilled cheese by dipping it into the Green Queen Dipping Sauce and indulging in all its crunchy, gooey, chewy goodness!

SPICY SOUTHWESTERN FALAFEL

MAKES 4 SERVINGS

Southwestern flavors always remind me of growing up in Arizona, constantly surrounded by so much bold, authentic food. While there's nothing like eating food prepared by people native to the culture, this combination of ingredients prepared in my own kitchen brings me all the joyful and nostalgic feels.

FALAFEL

One 15-ounce can chickpeas, drained and rinsed
1 small red onion, roughly chopped
4 garlic cloves, roughly chopped
1 cup chopped fresh cilantro
1 cup roughly chopped baby kale
1 to 2 teaspoons chili powder, to taste
1½ teaspoons ground cumin
1 teaspoon paprika
½ teaspoon kosher salt, or to taste

2 tablespoons olive oil, plus more for brushing
½ cup oat flour, store-bought or homemade (see right)

ACCOMPANIMENTS

Fluffy Gluten-Free Flatbreads (page 220)
Sliced tomatoes
Quick-Pickled Red Onions (page 129)
Raw greens (like lettuce or arugula)
Any additional veggies or sprouts you'd like
Lime wedges
Chipotle Tahini Sauce (page 235)

1. Preheat the oven to 400°F. Line a sheet pan with parchment paper.

2. To make the falafel: In a food processor, combine the chickpeas, onion, garlic, cilantro, kale, chili powder, cumin, paprika, salt, and 2 tablespoons olive oil and pulse until well incorporated, leaving a little bit of chunkiness. Add the oat flour and pulse until mixed in.

3. Transfer the mixture to a large bowl and form into a ball. Pull off 1- to 2-tablespoon chunks of the mixture and form into smaller balls, flattening each to ½-inch thickness.

4. Place the falafel balls on the prepared sheet pan and lightly brush the tops with olive oil.

5. Bake for 15 minutes, then carefully turn the falafel balls over with a spatula. Bake 10 to 15 minutes more, until golden brown.

6. To assemble: Place the falafel balls in flatbreads and stuff the flatbreads with tomatoes, onions, raw greens, and any other veggies you'd like. Drizzle with chipotle tahini sauce. Enjoy!

OAT YEAH! HOW TO MAKE OAT FLOUR

With the same quality as store-bought, oat flour made from scratch is wonderfully easy and inexpensive.

Place 1 to 2 cups old-fashioned rolled oats in a food processor or blender. Secure the lid and process or blend on high speed until the oats turn into a fine powder or flour. Store in an airtight container for up to 3 months. That's it!

BBQ SWEET POTATO TORTIZZA

MAKES 4 SERVINGS

This is an OG recipe of mine that I've been making for years at home and in my nonprofit summer camps with hundreds of campers. It's a nontraditional pizza that's sweet and smoky and can be loaded with any veggies you love!

2 medium to large sweet potatoes
Two 8-inch flour tortillas (can be gluten-free or regular flour)
1 cup Sweet and Smoky BBQ Sauce (page 237)
1 cup thinly sliced red onion

1 cup sliced mushrooms of your choice (I love using shiitake and maitake)
1 cup sliced yellow and orange bell peppers
Any seasonal veggies you love! (see chart on page 130 for ideas)
Chopped fresh cilantro

1. Preheat the oven to 400°F. Line a baking sheet with foil.

2. Lay the sweet potatoes on the prepared pan and roast them for 20 to 40 minutes, depending on their size, until soft. Remove the sweet potatoes (leave the oven on) and when cool enough to handle, peel and mash them.

3. Line a sheet pan with parchment paper. Lay a tortilla on the sheet pan and spread the mashed sweet potato evenly over its surface. Top with the second tortilla.

4. Spread the BBQ sauce all over the top of the tortilla, making sure to coat the edges so they don't curl when baking later. Lay the onion, mushrooms, bell peppers, and any other veggies you like on top. Bake for about 10 minutes to heat through.

5. Top with cilantro, slice, and enjoy this yummy remixed pizza!

FLUFFY GLUTEN-FREE FLATBREADS

MAKES 8 FLATBREADS

Eating mostly gluten-free, I usually miss the doughy, soft, and pillowy mouth-feel of wheat breads . . . but this flatbread is honestly the closest I've come to experiencing that gluten happiness without getting a stomachache later. This flatbread can be layered and stuffed a million ways and serves as a great base for enjoying something sweet or savory!

3½ cups Bob's Red Mill Gluten-Free 1 to 1 Baking Flour or other 1:1 gluten-free flour, plus more as needed
1 teaspoon kosher salt
1 to 2 teaspoons garlic powder, to taste
1½ tablespoons baking powder
¾ cup room-temperature water
½ cup unsweetened oat milk

1 vegan egg (I use Bob's Red Mill egg replacer)
3 tablespoons olive oil, for brushing

OPTIONAL (BUT HIGHLY RECOMMENDED) TOPPINGS
Savory: Olive oil and chopped fresh parsley
Sweet: Pure maple syrup and ground cinnamon

1. In a large bowl, combine the flour, salt, garlic powder, and baking powder. Whisk to combine.

2. In a medium bowl, whisk the water, oat milk, vegan egg, and oil. Add the wet mixture to the flour mixture and stir until you have a thick dough.

3. Use your hands to mix further until you have a ball of soft yet slightly sticky dough. If it is dry and flaky, add water 1 tablespoon at a time to help the ball come together. If the dough is sticking to your fingers, add about 2 table-spoons of flour at a time.

4. Place the dough ball on a heavily floured surface and gently roll the ball in the flour. Using a serrated knife, cut the dough in half. Roll both halves into two separate balls and cut each in half. Roll those 4 pieces into smaller balls and cut each in half as well. Roll into 8 total dough balls.

5. Line a sheet pan with parchment paper.

6. Knead each ball with your hands until it is soft yet sturdy and flexible. Place a ball of dough on the floured surface and gently press it into a flat round. Flip

the flatbread round and press to flatten a bit more. Continue to flip and press into a 5- to 7-inch flatbread round. Gently dust off any excess flour and transfer to the prepared sheet pan. Repeat to flatten the rest of the dough balls.

7. Heat a large skillet over medium heat.

8. Lightly brush a flatbread with olive oil on both sides. Gently place the flatbread in the skillet and cook until a little puffy, about 1 minute. Use a spatula to flip and cook for another 30 seconds or so. Transfer to a plate or serving dish and cover with a clean kitchen towel to keep soft and warm. Repeat the oiling and cooking process for the remaining flatbreads.

9. Enjoy these ASAP when they're nice and warm with a brush of olive oil and sprinkle of parsley or a drizzle of maple syrup and dash of cinnamon.

SUN-DRIED TOMATO AND WALNUT TACOS

MAKES 4 SERVINGS

I love making these lettuce wraps on days when it's just too hot for cooked food. They're light and refreshing but still somehow super filling! This is a great, sharable dish to make when you're just chilling with family and friends.

2 cups raw walnuts
½ cup sun-dried tomatoes in olive oil, drained
¼ cup tamari
1 tablespoon ground cumin
1 tablespoon onion powder
2 teaspoons chili powder
½ to 1 teaspoon cayenne pepper
¼ cup roughly chopped fresh cilantro
Romaine or butter lettuce leaves

OPTIONAL (BUT HIGHLY RECOMMENDED) TOPPINGS
Cilantro Aioli (page 237)
Halved cherry tomatoes
Sliced red onion
Sliced jalapeño rounds
Fresh cilantro
Your favorite vegetables

1. In a food processor, combine the walnuts, sun-dried tomatoes, tamari, cumin, onion powder, chili powder, cayenne, and cilantro and pulse 2 to 4 times. The goal is to have a texture that is crunchy and chewy, not mushy. Set aside.

2. Build the tacos by filling a lettuce "shell" with the walnut mixture and your choice of toppings.

CHICKPEA OF THE SEA SANDWICH

MAKES 4 SERVINGS

This sandwich recipe is actually one of the first recipes I made when I went vegan in 2014! I had recently learned that dulse (a type of seaweed) is a magical transformer and wonderful plant-based way to get a taste of the sea, with no fish harmed in the making. I was throwing it on everything to make it taste "fishy"!

4½ cups drained canned chickpeas (from about three 15.5-ounce cans)
3 garlic cloves, roughly chopped
2 tablespoons dulse flakes
½ to 1 tablespoon grated lemon zest, to taste
1 to 2 teaspoons freshly ground black pepper, to taste
1½ teaspoons Himalayan pink salt, or to taste
1 teaspoon paprika
½ cup plus 2 tablespoons vegan mayo

½ cup chopped fresh parsley
½ cup diced radishes
½ cup finely diced red onion
Your favorite bread, toasted

OPTIONAL (BUT HIGHLY RECOMMENDED) TOPPINGS
Sliced radishes
Sprouts (I love alfalfa and sunflower sprouts!)
Sliced beefsteak tomatoes

1. In a food processor, combine 4 cups of the chickpeas, the garlic, dulse, lemon zest, pepper, salt, paprika, and 2 tablespoons of the mayo. Pulse 3 to 5 times, until the chickpea mixture is mostly pasty and slightly chunky. Taste and adjust the seasoning as needed.

2. Transfer the pulsed chickpea mix to a large bowl and add the remaining ½ cup whole chickpeas, the remaining ½ cup mayo, the parsley, radishes, and red onion and mix well to combine.

3. Spread ¾ to 1 cup of the chickpea mixture on each sandwich. If desired, top the sandwiches with the veg of your choice! Pack it for lunch or enjoy at home!

TANDOORI SPICED SWEET POTATO TACOS

MAKES 4 TO 6 SERVINGS

If I could eat only Indian or Mexican food for the rest of my life, I would honestly be perfectly content. This fusion taco is inspired by both of these bold and deeply dimensional cuisines that I love . . . and are even better together!

SWEET POTATOES
2 tablespoons olive oil
2 medium sweet potatoes (peeled or unpeeled), cut into bite-size chunks
1 tablespoon garlic powder
1 tablespoon tandoori masala
1 to 2 teaspoons garam masala, to taste
2 teaspoons onion powder
Kosher salt and freshly ground black pepper

BLACK BEANS
1 tablespoon olive oil
2 or 3 garlic cloves, minced
One 15-ounce can black beans, drained and rinsed
Kosher salt and freshly ground black pepper

CORN SLAW
1 cup corn kernels, frozen or cut from 1 to 2 ears
1 cup shredded red cabbage
½ cup shredded peeled carrots
2 scallions, chopped
¼ cup chopped fresh cilantro leaves
2 tablespoons olive oil
1 tablespoon fresh lime juice
1 tablespoon pure maple syrup
½ tablespoon distilled white vinegar
Kosher salt
1 tablespoon chopped fresh parsley

TACO ASSEMBLY
8 to 12 soft white or yellow corn tortillas
Cumin-Herb Yogurt Sauce (page 236)
Mint and parsley leaves (optional)

1. To make the sweet potatoes: Preheat the oven to 450°F. Lightly oil a sheet pan with 1 tablespoon of the olive oil.

2. Place the sweet potato chunks on the sheet pan and drizzle with the remaining olive oil. Sprinkle the sweet potatoes with the garlic powder, tandoori masala, garam masala, onion powder, and salt and pepper to taste and toss to coat. Roast the potatoes for 25 to 30 minutes, until soft when pierced with a fork. Set aside.

3. To make the black beans: In a small saucepan, heat the olive oil over medium-high heat. Add the garlic and sauté for 2 minutes, or until aromatic. Stir in the black beans, mix in salt and pepper to taste, and cook for 3 minutes to completely warm through. Set aside.

4. To make the corn slaw: In a medium bowl, combine the corn, cabbage, carrots, scallions, and cilantro. In a small bowl, whisk together the olive oil, lime juice, maple syrup, vinegar, salt to taste, and the parsley. Pour the dressing over the corn slaw and toss until evenly coated.

5. To assemble the tacos: Warm the tortillas one at a time in a dry nonstick pan for 15 to 30 seconds. Flip with tongs or a spatula and heat for another 15 to 30 seconds. Repeat this process with all of your tortillas. Fill each warm tortilla with sweet potatoes, black beans, corn slaw, a drizzle of cumin-herb yogurt sauce, and fresh herbs if you'd like! Enjoy!

KOREAN JACKFRUIT SLOPPY JILL

MAKES 4 TO 6 SERVINGS

For a while I only experienced jackfruit as really soggy and not very "pulled pork" like. So, I wasn't really sure if I was a fan. But after doing some experimenting, I discovered that, like just about anything, it's all in the cooking method and making sure that any sauce or liquid the jackfruit is cooked in is almost entirely absorbed. This Sloppy Jill is a little sweet, a little spicy, a little chewy, and perfectly juicy. Paired with a sesame slaw, it is a great sandwich with both fun textures and bold flavors!

JACKFRUIT

¾ cup coconut sugar
¾ cup reduced-sodium tamari
¼ cup vegetable broth
1 tablespoon rice vinegar
1½ tablespoons sambal oelek or sriracha
1½ teaspoons toasted sesame oil
2 teaspoons grated fresh ginger
5 garlic cloves, finely grated or pressed
1 tablespoon cornstarch
Two 20-ounce cans young green jackfruit in brine
1 tablespoon olive oil
1 scallion, thinly sliced

SESAME SLAW

1 medium red bell pepper, thinly sliced
¼ small red cabbage, thinly sliced
1 scallion, thinly sliced
¼ cup chopped fresh cilantro
1 tablespoon toasted sesame oil
2 teaspoons rice vinegar
1 teaspoon minced fresh ginger
1 teaspoon kosher salt
1 tablespoon white sesame seeds

TO SERVE

Vegan mayo
8 to 12 ciabatta rolls, toasted
Thinly sliced fresh basil leaves

1. To prepare the jackfruit: In a small saucepan, combine the coconut sugar, tamari, broth, vinegar, sambal oelek, sesame oil, ginger, and garlic. Bring to a boil over high heat.

2. Meanwhile, in a small bowl, combine the cornstarch and 1 tablespoon water and mix until smooth.

3. When the sauce is boiling, add the cornstarch mixture and whisk until thick. Remove from the heat and set the sauce aside.

4. Rinse, drain, and thoroughly dry the jackfruit with paper towels. Remove and discard any hard seeds. Heat a large skillet over medium heat and add the olive oil. Add the jackfruit and toss in the oil. Cook for 2 to 3 minutes, until the jackfruit is lightly golden.

5. Add the prepared sauce and sliced scallion. Toss to coat the jackfruit, then reduce the heat to medium-low. Cover and simmer, stirring occasionally, for about 20 minutes, or until slightly cooked down.

6. Grab two forks and shred the jackfruit as you would pulled pork or chicken. Stir well, uncover, and cook for 10 minutes, or until most liquid has been absorbed. Remove from the heat and set aside.

7. To make the sesame slaw: In a large bowl, toss together the bell pepper, cabbage, scallion, and cilantro. In a small bowl, whisk together the sesame oil, rice vinegar, ginger, and salt until well blended. Drizzle the mixture over the veggies, add the sesame seeds, and toss to coat using your hands or tongs.

8. To serve: Spread vegan mayo on the tops and bottoms of the toasted ciabatta. On the bottom buns, layer ¼ cup jackfruit, then 1 to 2 tablespoons of the slaw. Garnish with slivered basil and add the top buns. Enjoy this irresistible Sloppy Jill!

JAMAICAN JERK BANH MI PIZZA

MAKES 4 SERVINGS

There's nothing more exciting than seeing several of your favorite dishes in one. It's a fusion mash-up of all the ingredients and flavors of a delicious banh mi sandwich thrown onto a pizza and topped with Jamaican jerk mushrooms. An unexpected combo that just works beautifully!

JERK MUSHROOMS

7½ ounces oyster mushrooms, cut into 1-inch slices

¾ cup Jamaican Jerk-ish Sauce (page 239)

QUICK-PICKLED CARROTS AND ONIONS

½ cup red wine vinegar

1 teaspoon sea salt

1 cup shredded peeled carrots

½ cup thinly sliced red onion

BANH MI SAUCE

1 teaspoon rice vinegar

1 teaspoon pure maple syrup

1 teaspoon toasted sesame oil

1 teaspoon tamari

1 teaspoon sambal oelek

CREAMY SRIRACHA MAYO

¼ cup vegan mayo

½ to 1 tablespoon fresh lime juice

½ tablespoon sriracha

½ to 1 teaspoon kosher salt

PIZZA

1 tablespoon olive oil

1 ball store-bought pizza dough

½ cup baby arugula

¼ cup thinly sliced fresh red chiles

⅓ cup thinly sliced cucumber

1. To prepare the mushrooms: In a medium bowl, combine the oyster mushrooms and jerk-ish sauce. Stir to coat the mushrooms evenly. Cover and refrigerate for at least 30 minutes and up to overnight.

2. To make the quick pickles: In a medium bowl, combine the vinegar and salt. Add the carrots and onion and refrigerate while you pull together the remaining recipe components.

3. To make the banh mi sauce: In a small bowl, whisk together the vinegar, maple syrup, sesame oil, tamari, and sambal oelek. Set aside.

4. To make the sriracha mayo: In a small bowl, whisk together the vegan mayo, lime juice, sriracha, and salt. Pour the sauce into a squeeze bottle and refrigerate until ready to use.

5. To make the pizza: Remove the marinated mushrooms from the fridge, drain off the marinade, and lightly pat them with paper towels to absorb any excess marinade.

6. In a medium skillet, heat the olive oil over medium-high heat. Add the mushrooms in a single layer and cook on one side for 2 minutes without stirring. Reduce the heat to medium, use a spatula to flip the mushrooms to the other side, and cook another 3 to 5 minutes, until the mushrooms are browned and slightly crispy. Remove from the heat and set aside.

7. Shape the pizza dough into a round or square and bake it according to the package directions. Spread the banh mi sauce over the hot pizza. Pop back into the oven and bake for 3 minutes, or until the sauce is mostly absorbed.

8. Top the pizza with pickled carrots and onions, jerk mushrooms, arugula, sliced chiles, and cucumbers. Drizzle some sriracha mayo on top, slice, and enjoy!

Sauces

CHIPOTLE TAHINI SAUCE

MAKES ABOUT 1½ CUPS

I love this simple sauce because it's great for spicing up a salad or bringing some roasted veggies to life. The hint of heat from the chipotle paired with the deep nuttiness of tahini makes for a really lovely addition to savory dishes like the Straight Fire Mac and Cheese (page 201).

½ cup tahini
2 teaspoons chipotle powder
1 tablespoon fresh lemon juice

4 garlic cloves, peeled
1 cup vegetable broth
Kosher salt to taste

In a small blender or food processor, combine all the ingredients and process until smooth. Cover and refrigerate in an airtight glass container for up to 6 days.

CILANTRO-TAHINI DRESSING

MAKES ABOUT 1½ CUPS

Bright and nutty, this dressing is a lovely addition to dishes with Southwestern flavors and ingredients, especially if you love cilantro just as much as I do (a lot!). It adds a wonderful pop of flavor to classic tacos and quesadillas.

¾ cup tahini
7 tablespoons water
5 tablespoons fresh lime juice
½ cup fresh cilantro

½ tablespoon diced jalapeño
2 garlic cloves, peeled
Kosher salt to taste

In a small blender or food processor, combine all the ingredients and process until smooth. Cover and refrigerate in an airtight glass container for up to 6 days.

MAPLE HARISSA DRESSING

MAKES ABOUT ⅓ CUP

This fiery dressing brings sweet and smoky flavors that meld beautifully with salads or bowls. It's delicious with seared tofu and especially with dried fruit like golden raisins or cherries—think about adding these components to your next bowl!

1 tablespoon harissa spice blend
1 tablespoon olive oil
2 tablespoons pure maple syrup
2 to 3 garlic cloves, peeled, to taste

2 tablespoons fresh orange juice
2 tablespoons fresh lemon juice
Kosher salt to taste

In a small blender or food processor, combine all the ingredients and blend until smooth and creamy. Cover and refrigerate in an airtight glass container for up to 1 week.

CUMIN-HERB YOGURT SAUCE

MAKES ABOUT 1 CUP

Refreshing and light, this sauce adds vibrancy to dishes with warming spices like smoked paprika, cumin, or turmeric!

¾ cup plant-based yogurt
2 to 3 tablespoons fresh lime juice, to taste
1½ to 2 teaspoons ground cumin, to taste
¼ cup mixed fresh mint and parsley leaves

1 teaspoon olive oil
Handful of fresh cilantro
Kosher salt and freshly ground black pepper to taste

In a small blender or food processor, combine all the ingredients and blend until smooth. Adjust the seasonings as desired. Cover and refrigerate in an airtight glass container for up to 6 days.

Tip: This sauce will thicken in the fridge. When thick, it's perfect for dolloping—but if you'd like to loosen the sauce, stir well and mix in water, 1 tablespoon at a time, until it reaches your desired consistency.

SWEET AND SMOKY BBQ SAUCE

MAKES ABOUT 1¼ CUP

Use this BBQ sauce (with pride in knowing there aren't any artificial sweeteners, colors, or preservatives added) as you would any store-bought BBQ sauce! It's great with plant proteins, on pizza or burritos, or as a unique spin on nachos!

1 cup ketchup (try to use a brand with minimal ingredients and no high-fructose corn syrup)
3 to 4 tablespoons pure maple syrup, to taste
2 tablespoons apple cider vinegar
2 tablespoons distilled white vinegar
1 tablespoon tamari

1 tablespoon yellow mustard
1 tablespoon paprika
1 tablespoon garlic powder
1 tablespoon onion powder
1 teaspoon chili powder
Kosher salt to taste

In a small blender or food processor, combine all the ingredients and blend until smooth (or whisk the ingredients in a medium bowl). Cover and refrigerate in an airtight glass container for up to 1 week.

CILANTRO AIOLI

MAKES A HEAPING ½ CUP

Herby, tangy deliciousness, perfect for spreading on sandwiches or as a dip for veggies.

¾ cup vegan mayo
2 tablespoons olive oil
2 tablespoons fresh lime juice
½ cup chopped fresh cilantro
2 large garlic cloves, peeled

Grated zest of 1 lime
1 teaspoon ground cumin
Kosher salt and freshly ground black pepper to taste

In a small blender or food processor, combine all the ingredients and blend until smooth and creamy. Adjust the seasonings as desired. Cover and refrigerate in an airtight glass container for up to 1 week.

5-SPICE SUNFLOWER SAUCE

MAKES ABOUT 1 CUP

A ridiculously creamy, sweet, salty, spicy, nutty sauce that pairs gorgeously with noodle stir-fries or as a dip for spring rolls!

⅓ cup plus 2 tablespoons sunflower seed butter
⅓ cup plus 2 tablespoons hot water
1 tablespoon tamari, soy sauce, or liquid aminos
1 tablespoon pure maple syrup
1 tablespoon fresh lime juice

1 tablespoon sriracha
3 medium garlic cloves, peeled
½ tablespoon brown rice miso paste
½ to 1 teaspoon Chinese 5-spice powder, to taste
Kosher salt to taste

In a small blender or food processor, combine all the ingredients and blend until smooth and creamy. Cover and refrigerate in an airtight glass container for up to 3 days.

GREEN QUEEN DIPPING SAUCE

MAKES ABOUT 1 CUP

My love for avocado only grows stronger with this sauce! Its avocado richness and layers of herb goodness make it destined for iconic dipping. Fantastic with Crunchy Mushroom Grilled Cheese (page 215), roasted potato wedges, or spread on toast.

1 medium avocado, halved and pitted
½ cup fresh basil leaves
2 scallions, chopped
2 large garlic cloves, peeled

½ cup olive oil
Juice of 1 lemon (3 to 4 tablespoons)
Kosher salt and freshly ground black pepper to taste

Scoop the avocado into a small blender or food processor. Add the remaining ingredients and blend until smooth and creamy. Cover and refrigerate in an airtight glass container for up to 3 days.

JAMAICAN JERK-ISH SAUCE

MAKES A LITTLE MORE THAN 1¼ CUPS

I call this a jerk-ish sauce because I can admit that authentic, straight-from-Jamaica jerk sauce just can't be replicated—but as a first-generation American, I feel like this one comes pretty close! With all of the traditional spices and elements (and a little less heat), this sauce is an approachable intro to a Jamaican staple.

1 medium yellow onion, roughly chopped
5 scallions, trimmed and roughly chopped
1 to 2 Scotch bonnet peppers (add more if you like heat!), seeded
6 to 8 garlic cloves, peeled
10 to 15 fresh thyme sprigs, stems removed
¼ cup plus 1 tablespoon rice vinegar
¼ cup tamari

2 tablespoons olive oil
Juice of ½ lime
1 tablespoon allspice berries
4 teaspoons grated fresh ginger
2 tablespoons coconut sugar
1 teaspoon ground nutmeg
Kosher salt to taste

In a blender, combine all the ingredients and blend until well incorporated and the sauce is a little chunky. Adjust the seasonings as needed. Cover and refrigerate in an airtight glass container for up to 1 week.

Treat
Yo' Self

GLUTEN-FREE CHAI-COCONUT BANANA BREAD

MAKES 7 TO 14 SLICES

I've always adored banana bread as a laid-back dessert (or breakfast!) with classic comfort. I had some fun with this recipe and added some chai-inspired spices and crystallized ginger for a little kick, texture, and chewiness.

Enjoy this bread as is or with vegan butter or jam, or refrigerate overnight and make it into French Toast Sticks (page 141) in the morning!

3 medium ripe bananas, mashed (about 1½ cups)
¾ cup unsweetened oat milk
1 teaspoon pure vanilla extract
3 tablespoons coconut oil, melted
2 tablespoons pure maple syrup
½ cup coconut sugar
1 tablespoon flaxseed meal
3½ teaspoons baking powder
2 teaspoons ground cinnamon
2 teaspoons ground ginger

¾ teaspoon sea salt
¼ teaspoon ground cardamom
½ teaspoon ground nutmeg
Pinch of ground cloves
1¼ cups almond flour
1¼ cups Bob's Red Mill Gluten-Free 1 to 1 Baking Flour or other 1:1 gluten-free flour
¾ cup gluten-free rolled oats
½ cup unsweetened shredded coconut
½ cup diced (¼-inch) crystallized ginger

1. Preheat the oven to 350°F. Line the bottom and all sides of a 9 × 9-inch baking pan with parchment paper.

2. In a large bowl, combine the mashed bananas, oat milk, 2½ tablespoons water, the vanilla, coconut oil, maple syrup, coconut sugar, flaxseed meal, baking powder, cinnamon, ground ginger, salt, cardamom, nutmeg, and cloves. Whisk well to combine. Add the almond flour, gluten-free flour, oats, shredded coconut, and crystallized ginger and stir until fully incorporated.

3. Spoon the banana bread batter into the prepared baking pan and bake for 1 hour 15 minutes, or until firm and golden brown on top. A knife should come out clean when inserted in the center. Let cool completely before slicing.

4. Place leftovers in a covered container for up 3 days. Freeze slices for longer-term storage.

STRAWBERRY-TAHINI-COCONUT COOKIES

MAKES 12 HUNKY COOKIES :)

Tahini + cookies = pure happiness. I love mixing tahini in with sweet and fruity ingredients! Its rich and roasty flavor pairs so well with the tanginess of the strawberries and deep nuttiness of the coconut sugar and flakes. It's delightful with a little bit of crunch on the outside and all the soft, melt-in-your-mouth goodness on the inside.

½ cup coconut oil, at room temperature, with a creamy and soft texture
½ cup tahini
¾ cup coconut sugar
¼ cup unsweetened oat milk, or other plant milk of your choice
1 teaspoon pure vanilla extract
1½ cups Bob's Red Mill Gluten-Free 1 to 1 Baking Flour or other 1:1 gluten-free flour

1 tablespoon cornstarch
1 teaspoon kosher salt
1 teaspoon ground cinnamon
½ teaspoon baking soda
½ teaspoon baking powder
1 cup medium-diced strawberries
¾ cup unsweetened coconut flakes
Flaky sea salt, such as Maldon

1. In a stand mixer using the whisk attachment (or in a large bowl and using a hand mixer), beat the coconut oil, tahini, and coconut sugar on medium speed for 5 minutes. Adjust the speed as needed to get the mixture smooth and creamy. Add the oat milk and vanilla and mix 1 minute or so to combine.

2. In a medium bowl, whisk together the flour, cornstarch, salt, cinnamon, baking soda, and baking powder.

3. Add the flour mixture to the tahini mixture and, using the flat beater attachment, mix on low speed until just fully incorporated. Fold in the diced strawberries and coconut flakes. Cover the dough and refrigerate for at least 30 minutes and up to overnight.

4. Preheat the oven to 350°F. Line a large baking sheet with parchment paper.

5. Use a standard ice cream scoop to scoop the dough into 12 chunky balls. Place them 2 to 3 inches apart on the prepared baking sheet.

6. Bake for 25 to 30 minutes, until the cookies have risen and are golden brown. Immediately sprinkle a little pinch of flaky salt on top of each cookie.

7. Because they're gluten-free, they'll be a little delicate at first, but letting them cool for 30 minutes on a rack and/or placing the cooled cookies in the fridge for at least 15 minutes helps them firm up perfectly. Devour these cookies and try *not* to be obsessed. ;)

PUMPKIN PIE SNICKERDOODLES

MAKES 14 COOKIES

I had to throw in a cookie recipe with all the holiday vibes! Nothing is better than making these cookies during fall and enjoying them with a glass of oat milk while watching *alllll* the Netflix holiday originals. Eleven out of ten, highly recommend doing this exact routine when you make these snickerdoodles!

8 tablespoons (1 stick) cold vegan butter
¾ cup coconut sugar
½ tablespoon pure maple syrup
1 teaspoon pure vanilla extract
½ teaspoon almond extract
⅓ cup canned unsweetened pumpkin puree

1½ cups Bob's Red Mill Gluten-Free 1 to 1 Baking Flour or other 1:1 gluten-free flour
½ teaspoon baking soda
½ teaspoon baking powder
1½ teaspoons pumpkin pie spice
¼ teaspoon Himalayan pink salt
Vegan white chocolate (optional), melted

1. Preheat the oven to 350°F. Line a baking sheet with parchment paper.

2. In a stand mixer (or in a large bowl and using a hand mixer), combine the vegan butter, coconut sugar, and maple syrup. Cream them together on high speed until fully incorporated. Add the vanilla, almond extract, and pumpkin puree and mix them in on medium-high speed. Detach the bowl from the mixer.

3. Using a wooden spoon, stir in the flour, baking soda, baking powder, pumpkin pie spice, and salt until all the ingredients are fully combined. The consistency of the cookie dough will be soft, slightly wet, and malleable—kind of like a softer Play-Doh.

4. To form each cookie, scoop out 1 to 1½ tablespoons of the dough and roll and flatten it with your hands. You can mark each cookie with the stamp of a fork if you'd like! Place the cookies on the prepared baking sheet with about 1 inch of space between them. (My cookies were ¼ to ½ inch thick and the dough makes around 14 cookies.)

5. Bake for 15 minutes, or until golden brown. Let cool on a baking rack for 15 to 30 minutes.

6. If desired, drizzle the cookies with melted vegan white chocolate. Enjoy and get your cozy on! (If you somehow have leftover cookies, store them in a zip-top bag or airtight container for up to 3 days.)

NUTTY CHERRY-COCONUT SOFT SERVE

MAKES 2 TO 4 SERVINGS . . .

DEPENDING ON HOW GOOD YOU ARE AT SHARING SOFT SERVE :)

Treat yourself to this simple, creamy, cool delight in 5 minutes or less! Just remember to freeze the coconut milk overnight first. . . .

One 13.5-ounce can full-fat coconut milk

¼ cup unsweetened oat milk

2 tablespoons pure maple syrup

1 medium/large banana, cut into 6 pieces and frozen

1 cup frozen cherries (about 20)

1 tablespoon cashew butter (or the nut/seed butter of your choice)

1 tablespoon coconut butter (optional)

¼ teaspoon ground cardamom, or to taste (this is a strong spice, though, so increase with caution!)

OPTIONAL (BUT HIGHLY RECOMMENDED) TOPPINGS

Coconut flakes

Fresh cherries

1. The night before you want to make the soft serve, pour the canned coconut milk into 12 wells of an ice cube tray. Freeze overnight.

2. Remove the cubes from the freezer 5 to 10 minutes before you make the soft serve.

3. In a high-powered blender or food processor, combine the coconut milk cubes, oat milk, maple syrup, banana, cherries, cashew butter, coconut butter (if using), and cardamom and blend until thick and smooth.

4. Divide the soft serve among bowls. If you want to pop all the way off, serve with coconut flakes and fresh cherries!

SHORTCUT SWEET POTATO PIE BOATS

MAKES 4 SERVINGS

Sweet potato pie is *iconic*. But who said icons can't get a makeover? Because I love sweet potato pie so much, I had to figure out a way to veganize the recipe and simplify the process while still maintaining the traditional feel and tastiness. Dealing with crust making is not my favorite activity, so I've turned the crust into a crumble and put the "sweet" in sweet potato by spicing up the inside and topping it all with a delicious and light dollop of coconut whip! These boats are easy to make, eat, and enjoy—and you technically don't even need a plate. ;)

TAHINI OAT CRUMBLE

Heaping ⅓ cup coconut sugar
¼ cup oat flour, store-bought or homemade (see page 217)
½ cup rolled oats (gluten-free if needed)
¼ cup almond flour
½ teaspoon ground cinnamon
Pinch of kosher salt
1 tablespoon tahini
⅓ cup vegan butter, melted

ROASTED SWEET POTATOES

4 small to medium sweet potatoes

2 tablespoons pure maple syrup
1 teaspoon pure vanilla extract
1½ teaspoons ground cinnamon
½ teaspoon ground ginger
Pinch of ground nutmeg

OPTIONAL (BUT HIGHLY RECOMMENDED) TOPPINGS

Vegan whipped topping (I recommend So Delicious Coco Whip or Soyatoo! Rice Whip)
Chopped raw pecans
Unsweetened shredded coconut

1. Preheat the oven to 350°F. Line a baking sheet with parchment paper.

2. To make the tahini oat crumble: In a medium bowl, combine the coconut sugar, oat flour, oats, almond flour, cinnamon, and salt. Add the tahini and melted vegan butter and mix until the texture of the mixture resembles wet sand.

3. Spread the crumble mix evenly on the prepared baking sheet. Bake for 6 to 8 minutes, until bubbling and wet. This is what you want! Remove from the oven but leave the oven on, and increase the temperature to 400°F.

4. Let the crumble cool for 30 minutes to 1 hour, mixing every now and then to break it up. As the mixture cools it will begin to harden and develop a chewy texture. Set aside.

5. Meanwhile, to roast the sweet potatoes: Line a sheet pan with foil. Pierce each sweet potato several times across the surface with a fork. Place the potatoes on the sheet pan and bake for 50 minutes to 1 hour, until soft and syrupy.

6. Cut down the middle of each potato with a paring knife. Let the potatoes cool for 10 to 15 minutes, until you can handle them comfortably.

7. Gently scoop the insides of the potatoes into a medium bowl, setting aside the skins for later. Add the maple syrup, vanilla, cinnamon, ginger, and nutmeg and use a wooden spoon to smash the potatoes and mix them well.

8. Spoon the spiced sweet potato mixture into the potato skins and top with tahini oat crumble. If desired, also top with whipped topping, chopped pecans, and shredded coconut. Enjoy! Each bite is filled with pure comfort!

AB&J SWIRL BROWNIES

MAKES 8 TO 10 BROWNIES

PB&J just got an upgrade! Almond butter with raspberry-ginger jam and chocolate is a heavenly combo that has changed the game for me. I'm not the biggest fan of chocolate, but these brownies have somehow turned into one of my top dessert recipes. They're beautifully balanced and have a wonderful fudginess that's to live for!

RASPBERRY-GINGER JAM

3 cups frozen raspberries

1 tablespoon grated fresh ginger

2 to 3 tablespoons pure maple syrup, to taste

BROWNIE BATTER

⅓ cup creamy almond butter

½ cup pure maple syrup

½ cup unsweetened cashew milk

1 teaspoon pure vanilla extract

2 cups super-fine almond flour

¼ cup oat flour, store-bought or homemade (see page 217)

¼ cup unsweetened cocoa powder

⅓ cup coconut sugar

1 teaspoon ground cinnamon

Pinch of kosher salt

¼ cup chopped vegan dark chocolate (any percentage you prefer! I like 70%)

¼ cup chopped roasted unsalted peanuts or almonds

SWIRL

¼ cup creamy almond butter

1. Preheat the oven 350°F. Line the bottom and all sides of an 8 × 8-inch baking pan with parchment paper.

2. In a medium saucepan, heat the frozen raspberries over low heat, stirring every now and then, until they fully thaw. Smash them gently with a fork until slightly chunky, then add the grated ginger and maple syrup and mix well to incorporate.

3. Bring the berry mixture to a boil, reduce the heat to medium-low, and simmer for 10 to 15 minutes, until the mixture has slightly thickened. Set aside to cool and place in the fridge to thicken until it is time to swirl your brownies.

4. To make the brownie batter: In a large bowl, stir together the almond butter, maple syrup, cashew milk, vanilla, almond flour, oat flour, cocoa, coconut sugar, cinnamon, and salt. Stir in the chocolate and peanuts.

5. To make the swirl: Scrape the brownie batter into the prepared pan and smooth the top with a silicone spatula. Spoon the raspberry-ginger jam and the almond butter in repeating lines across the surface of the brownie batter. Use a butter knife or chopstick and gently drag it through the almond butter and raspberry jam lines to create any design you'd like (swirls, diagonal stripes, and so on).

6. Bake for 25 to 30 minutes, until the top is slightly crackled and a toothpick inserted in the center comes out with crumbs sticking to it.

7. Let cool in the pan for about 1 hour. Slice gently into 8 to 10 brownies and enjoy these decadent bites of chocolate happiness!

8. Store any leftover jam in an airtight glass container in the fridge for up to 7 days.

GLOWED-UP FRUITY QUINOA CRUMBLE

MAKES 4 TO 6 SERVINGS

Fun fact: This is the glowed-up version of a quinoa crumble recipe I made on the *Rachael Ray* show when I was twelve! It's now a vegan, refined sugar–free, and gluten-free remix that has lovely summer fruit and toasty spices!

Coconut oil, for the baking dish

BLUEBERRY-APRICOT FILLING

½ cup fresh blueberries

6 fresh apricots (unpeeled), chopped

¼ cup coconut sugar

3 tablespoons almond flour

1 teaspoon ground cinnamon

¼ teaspoon ground cardamom

½ tablespoon cornstarch

CRUMBLE

½ cup coconut sugar

½ cup almond flour

½ cup uncooked quinoa, rinsed

½ cup roughly chopped thinly sliced almonds

3 tablespoons hemp hearts

¼ teaspoon ground nutmeg

½ cup solid coconut oil

OPTIONAL ACCOMPANIMENTS

Vegan whipped topping (I recommend So Delicious Coco Whip or Soyatoo! Rice Whip)

Vegan ice cream

1. Preheat the oven to 375°F. Lightly oil a shallow 3-quart baking dish with coconut oil.

2. To make the blueberry-apricot filling: In a medium bowl, combine the fruit, sugar, almond flour, cinnamon, cardamom, and cornstarch and mix well. Spoon the filling into the prepared baking dish and set aside.

3. To make the crumble: In another medium bowl, combine the coconut sugar, almond flour, quinoa, slivered almonds, hemp hearts, and nutmeg, Add the coconut oil and use your hands to work it in until you have a crumbly mixture that comes together a bit.

4. Evenly top the fruit filling with the crumble. Bake for 45 to 55 minutes, until the top is golden brown with bubbling fruit peeking through.

5. Enjoy solo, or with whipped topping or ice cream!

CASHEW "CHEESECAKE" SQUARES

MAKES ABOUT 12 SQUARES

For as long as I can remember, cheesecake has been my most favorite dessert ever. So, when I decided to go vegan, one of the first things I wanted to experiment with was a dairy-free cheesecake. I've tried using tofu, plant-based cream cheese, and other interesting ingredients . . . but a cashew base is just perfectly rich and creamy. These squares are filled with delicious nostalgia and could definitely compete with your traditional cheesecake.

Note: You'll want to plan ahead for this recipe! The cashews need to soak overnight before you make the cheesecake, and then the cheesecake needs to be frozen for 6 hours to overnight. It will be worth it!

1½ cups raw cashews

CRUST

½ cup raw almonds (or nut of your choice, such as cashews or peanuts)
¾ cup rolled oats (gluten-free if needed)
1 cup pitted Medjool or Deglet Noor dates
½ cup fresh blueberries or diced fruit of your choice (such as raspberries, blackberries, strawberries)
1 teaspoon ground cinnamon
¼ teaspoon ground cardamom

"CHEESECAKE" BATTER

½ cup full-fat coconut milk
⅓ cup pure maple syrup
3 tablespoons coconut oil, melted and cooled
2 tablespoons fresh lemon juice
1 tablespoon grated orange zest
1 teaspoon pure vanilla extract
¼ teaspoon Himalayan pink salt

OPTIONAL BLUE/LAVENDER/PINK SWIRL

1½ teaspoons colored powder: butterfly pea flower powder (for blue), pitaya or beet powder (for pink)

1. In a bowl, fully cover the cashews in water and soak overnight in the fridge.

2. Line the bottom and all sides of a 9 × 9-inch baking pan with parchment paper (or use a springform pan).

3. To make the crust: In a food processor, pulse together the almonds, oats, dates, blueberries, cinnamon, and cardamom until well incorporated. The mixture should be thick and stick together when pressed.

4. Evenly press the crust over the bottom of the lined pan. Freeze for 20 minutes.

5. To make the batter: Drain the cashews and transfer to a large high-powered blender (see Tip). Add the coconut milk, maple syrup, coconut oil, lemon juice, orange zest, vanilla, and salt and blend until smooth and creamy.

6. If you want your cheesecake squares to have swirls, set aside most of the cheesecake batter in a large bowl, leaving ¼ cup in the blender. Add the butterfly pea flower powder, pitaya powder, or beet powder in the blender and blend until smooth. Transfer the colored batter to a small bowl.

7. Remove the prepared crust from the freezer and pour the cheesecake batter over the crust, spreading it evenly. To add swirls, drop small dollops of the colored batter across the top of the cheesecake and swirl them with a toothpick or chopstick.

8. Freeze the cheesecake for at least 6 hours and up to overnight.

9. Let sit at room temperature for 20 minutes before serving.

Tip: For this recipe, you'll need to use a high-powered blender to ensure the cashews can be fully broken down and blended to achieve the creamiest possible "cheesecake" consistency.

POWER NOMS
Bites with Power

Now, we've all heard the saying "You are what you eat." This message not only applies to our physical bodies, but to our minds as well. Depending on what foods are on our plates, our symptoms of stress or anxiety can be either heightened or lowered. As you try a few of these recipes every now and then or make other food choices at home or out and about, I want you to think about how each meal makes you feel. This mindfulness is just as important as what you fuel your body with. When you can tune in, you are able to determine what does and doesn't work for you. Take note when you eat something and feel a little sluggish or incredibly upbeat and energized. The more we do this, the closer we get to understanding how best to nourish ourselves.

Here in the Power Noms chapter, you'll find recipes with specific and intentional benefits for your mind and body! These recipes are all about supporting you in rebalancing, reenergizing, and becoming grounded or calm.

CHILL DOUGH (GOLDEN OAT COOKIE DOUGH BITES)

MAKES 8 TO 10 BITES

When you just need to chill, take a bite out of these bites! They contain two key ingredients that can help reduce stress and anxiety and elevate mood. Turmeric contains an active ingredient called curcumin that can help diminish anxiety by reducing inflammation and lowering the effects of stress. And dark chocolate contains high amounts of tryptophan, which helps the body produce more serotonin, a fancy name for a mood-boosting chemical that sends happy signals to the brain.

½ cup oat flour, store-bought or homemade (see page 217)
½ cup rolled oats (gluten-free if needed)
2 tablespoons white sesame seeds
1 teaspoon ground cinnamon
¾ teaspoon ground turmeric

¼ teaspoon kosher salt
Pinch of freshly ground black pepper
⅓ cup vegan dark chocolate chips
½ cup sunflower seed butter
3 tablespoons pure maple syrup
½ teaspoon pure vanilla extract

1. In a medium bowl, combine the oat flour, oats, sesame seeds, cinnamon, turmeric, salt and pepper. Add the sunflower seed butter, maple syrup, and vanilla and stir well until the mixture is smooth. The consistency of the dough should be slightly sticky; it will hold together when pressed.

2. Scoop ½ to 1 tablespoon of dough out of the bowl and roll it into a ball. Set the ball on a parchment paper–lined plate or baking dish. Repeat to make the rest of the balls.

3. Freeze for 10 to 15 minutes, remove, and enjoy! Store in the fridge for up to 1 week.

CHOCOLATE MACA POPCORN

MAKES 4 SERVINGS

Popcorn is often delightful to eat but rarely loaded with powerful ingredients. Because it's a blank canvas, it's perfect for throwing in all kinds of nourishing powders and spices. Here we use cocoa for the antioxidants, maca for boosting energy and mood, and cinnamon and cardamom for anti-inflammatory properties that help our bodies fight infections.

1 tablespoon coconut oil
½ cup white popcorn kernels
½ cup pure maple syrup
2 tablespoons unsweetened cocoa powder

1 teaspoon maca powder
1½ teaspoons ground cinnamon
¼ teaspoon ground cardamom

1. Preheat the oven to 250°F. Line a large sheet pan with parchment paper.

2. In a large pot, melt the coconut oil over medium heat. Add the popcorn kernels, cover, and shake to make sure all the kernels are coated. When the kernels start popping, put oven mitts on both hands and grab the pot handles to shake the popcorn every 15 seconds or so. When the popping starts to slow down, remove the pan from the heat and wait until the kernels stop popping. Pour the popcorn into a large bowl.

3. In a small saucepan, bring the maple syrup to a boil over medium heat. The syrup will bubble and look foamy. Boil for 3 minutes.

4. Pour the heated maple syrup over the popcorn and add the cocoa powder, maca, cinnamon, and cardamom. With a wooden spoon, stir to coat the popcorn.

5. Spread the popcorn evenly across the prepared sheet pan and bake for 25 to 30 minutes, until the popcorn is slightly firm and crisp. Let it cool for 2 to 3 minutes to fully crunch up. Enjoy as the perfect daytime pick-me-up or movie snack!

6. Store the popcorn in an airtight container at room temperature and it will keep for about 2 weeks—if you don't finish it before then!

FEEL BETTER BERRY BARS

MAKES 12 BARS

If you're feeling a little stressed or anxious, treat yourself to these soothing and delicious bars. There are three main ingredients that contribute to its calming properties: Brazil nuts, which are high in selenium, can help improve mood; potassium-rich pumpkin seeds can reduce stress; and antioxidant-packed blueberries can help provide anxiety relief.

NUT AND SEED BASE

1 cup raw almonds
½ cup raw Brazil nuts
½ cup raw pumpkin seeds
½ cup unsweetened shredded coconut
2 tablespoons maca powder
1 cup golden raisins
2 tablespoons sunflower seed butter
2 tablespoons unsweetened oat milk, plus more as needed

BERRY-BEET TOP LAYER

2 cups frozen blueberries
1 tablespoon beet powder

2 to 3 tablespoons pure maple syrup, to taste
2 tablespoons coconut oil, melted
½ cup unsweetened finely shredded coconut
¼ cup chia seeds
1 tablespoon sunflower seed butter
½ cup raw cashews, soaked in hot water for at least 10 minutes
¼ cup unsweetened oat milk
1 teaspoon pure vanilla extract

OPTIONAL TOPPINGS

Unsweetened shredded coconut
Raw pumpkin seeds
Raw slivered almonds

1. Line the bottom and sides of a 9 × 9-inch baking pan with parchment paper.

2. To make the nut and seed base: In a food processor, combine the almonds, Brazil nuts, pumpkin seeds, coconut, maca powder, raisins, sunflower seed butter, and 2 tablespoons oat milk and blend until crumbly and sticky. If the mixture is a bit dry and doesn't stick to itself, add more oat milk 1 tablespoon at a time and blend.

3. Pour the mixture into the prepared baking pan and press into an even layer across the bottom. Freeze while you make the top layer!

4. To make the berry-beet top layer: In a food processor, combine the blueberries, beet powder, maple syrup, coconut oil, coconut, chia seeds, sunflower seed butter, drained cashews, oat milk, and vanilla and blend until smooth and thick.

5. Remove the pan from the freezer and pour the berry-beet layer over the nut and seed base. Smooth across the surface with a spatula. Freeze for 30 minutes to 1 hour, until set.

6. Remove from the freezer and, if desired, top with coconut shreds, pumpkin seeds, and almond slivers. Slice into 12 bars and enjoy! You can store the bars in the fridge for 3 days or the freezer for up to 1 month.

KEY LIME AVOCADO MOUSSE CUPS

MAKES 2 SERVINGS

These creamy and mellow avocado mousse cups are packed with magnesium, antioxidants, and healthy fats—which help to reduce the symptoms of anxiety. Magnesium naturally calms the nervous system and aids the brain in stabilizing mood, while antioxidants and healthy fats help improve circulation, which = better blood flow to the brain.

KEY LIME AVOCADO MOUSSE
2 avocados, halved and pitted
3 to 4 tablespoons pure maple syrup, to taste
2 tablespoons fresh lime juice
1 teaspoon pure vanilla extract
Pinch of sea salt

RAWNOLA CRUMBLE
¾ cup rolled oats (gluten-free if needed)
⅓ cup raw pistachios
¼ cup raw sunflower seeds

¼ cup raw pumpkin seeds
3 tablespoons coconut oil, melted
3 tablespoons pure maple syrup
1 teaspoon pure vanilla extract
¼ teaspoon fine sea salt

OPTIONAL (BUT HIGHLY RECOMMENDED) TOPPINGS
Extra rawnola crumble
Kiwi slices
Grated lime zest

1. To make the mousse: Scoop the avocados into a food processor. Add 3 tablespoons maple syrup, the lime juice, the vanilla, and the salt and blend until smooth and creamy. Taste and add more maple syrup as desired. Blend again if needed and set aside in the fridge to chill.

2. To make the rawnola crumble: In a food processor, combine the oats, pistachios, sunflower seeds, pumpkin seeds, coconut oil, maple syrup, vanilla, and salt and process until slightly sticky and crumbly.

3. Grab two small cups and add ¼ cup rawnola crumble to each. Top with 3 tablespoons avocado mousse and layer with another ¼ cup crumble. Top each cup with about 2 tablespoons of the remaining mousse and any toppings you'd like (including leftover rawnola crumble). Enjoy these rich and creamy cups as a calming, good-for-you treat!

MATCHA GOJI CRISPY RICE BARS

MAKES 16 BARS

These earthy, sweet, and toasty bars are the ideal energizer, thanks to powerful seeds, goji berries, and matcha powder, which bring a boost of antioxidants, fiber, and omega-3 fats for a slow and steady release of energy.

½ cup sunflower seed butter
½ cup pure maple syrup
2 teaspoons pure vanilla extract
¼ teaspoon sea salt
2 cups puffed brown rice cereal
½ cup unsweetened shredded coconut

¼ cup flaxseeds
2 tablespoons hemp hearts
2 tablespoons chia seeds
¼ cup goji berries
2 teaspoons matcha powder

1. Line the bottom and sides of a 9 × 9-inch baking pan with parchment paper.

2. In a small saucepan, combine the sunflower seed butter, maple syrup, vanilla, and salt. Stir over medium-low heat until melted, then remove from the heat.

3. In a large bowl, combine the cereal, coconut, flaxseed, hemp hearts, chia seeds, goji berries, and matcha powder, stirring to make sure everything is coated with matcha powder. Pour the sunflower seed butter mixture over the crispy rice mixture and stir until well combined.

4. Scoop the mixture into the lined pan and press it down firmly until it is tightly packed. Pop into the fridge to cool and set for about 30 minutes. Cut into squares and enjoy!

CURRY CRUNCH TRAIL MIX

MAKES ABOUT 7 CUPS

This ridiculously easy trail mix is the perfect grab 'n' go snack for sustained energy throughout the day! Grab a handful and get nourished by fiber, protein, and energy-boosting vitamins and minerals like iron, B vitamins, and manganese.

1 cup chopped raw almonds
1 cup chopped raw cashews
1 cup raw pumpkin seeds
1 cup raw sunflower seeds
½ cup sesame seeds
1 cup chopped dried apricots

1 cup golden raisins
1 tablespoon coconut sugar
1 tablespoon mild curry powder
1 tablespoon red pepper flakes
1 teaspoon sea salt

1. In a large bowl, stir together all the ingredients.

2. Devour raw or, to cook, preheat the oven to 375°F. Line a sheet pan with parchment paper.

3. Spread evenly on the prepared sheet pan and roast for 10 minutes, until golden brown and toasty. Enjoy as a go-to energizing snack!

KNOCKOUT NIGHTTIME COOKIES

MAKES 6 COOKIES

Help your body wind down in the evenings with these tasty and calming cookies. Have a cookie (or two!) a couple hours before going to bed to get in all the natural melatonin (which helps to balance our sleep cycles) from the almonds and cherries!

½ cup mashed banana (from about 1 medium)
2 tablespoons almond butter
½ cup unsweetened shredded coconut
½ cup chopped raw walnuts
½ cup dried cherries

⅓ cup rolled oats (gluten-free if needed)
¼ cup flaxseeds
1 tablespoon chia seeds
1 teaspoon pure vanilla extract
1 teaspoon ground cinnamon
½ teaspoon ground ginger

1. Preheat the oven to 350°F. Line a sheet pan with parchment paper.

2. In a large bowl, stir together the banana, almond butter, coconut, walnuts, cherries, oats, flaxseeds, chia seeds, vanilla, cinnamon, and ginger until thoroughly combined. The batter will be moist.

3. For each cookie, roll 2 tablespoons of the mixture into a ball and place on the prepared baking sheet, gently flattening the top with the palm of your hand. Bake for 12 to 15 minutes, until golden.

4. Cool on a wire rack and grab a cookie! The cookies keep in an airtight container for up to 1 week.

Hug-in-a-Mug
Drinks

COCONUT GOLDEN MILK

MAKES 1 SERVING

With the powers of cinnamon, turmeric, and ginger, Coconut Golden Milk is anti-inflammatory, immunity-boosting, and detoxifying. It's the perfect drink to start or end your day wrapped in rich, golden goodness.

1¼ cups full-fat coconut milk (from one 13.5-ounce can)
½ tablespoon coconut oil
1 teaspoon pure vanilla extract
½ teaspoon ground cinnamon

¾ teaspoon ground turmeric
Pinch of ground cardamom
¼ teaspoon ground ginger
Pinch of freshly ground black pepper
1 to 2 tablespoons pure maple syrup, to taste

1. In a small saucepan, combine the coconut milk, coconut oil, vanilla, cinnamon, turmeric, cardamom, ginger, and pepper. Heat over medium-high heat for about 3 minutes, stirring frequently, until warm and simmering.

2. Whisk in the maple syrup, taste, and adjust the sweetness if necessary.

3. Pour into a mug and sip to slow down and savor the flavor.

SPICED MAPLE MASALA HOT COCOA

MAKES 1 SERVING

This recipe gives the ultimate cozy drink a powerful remix! The heart-healthy and mood-boosting properties of cocoa combined with iron, calcium, and vitamin C–loaded maca, an anti-inflammatory, digestion-boosting superfood, make for an epic drink with a nourishing kick.

1¼ cups unsweetened oat milk
2 tablespoons unsweetened cocoa powder
2 to 3 tablespoons pure maple syrup, to taste
1 teaspoon maca powder
¼ teaspoon ground cinnamon
¼ teaspoon garam masala

Pinch of ground turmeric
Pinch of chipotle powder (optional)
Pinch of kosher salt
1 teaspoon pure vanilla extract
½ tablespoon coconut oil

In a small saucepan, bring the oat milk to a simmer over medium-high heat. Add the cocoa and maple syrup and whisk until smooth. Add the maca powder, cinnamon, garam masala, turmeric, and chipotle powder (if using). Simmer for 2 minutes, whisking constantly. Stir in the salt, vanilla, and coconut oil, pour into a mug, and enjoy!

PINK SUNRISE LATTE

MAKES 1 SERVING

This latte is not only gorgeous, but a powerhouse with brain- and body-boosting nitrates (from the beets), which stimulate blood and oxygen flow in the brain, muscles, and respiratory system. It's the perfect drink for when you want to re-energize and enter your day with some power!

1½ teaspoons beet powder
½ teaspoon ground cinnamon
½ teaspoon ground ginger
Pinch of ground cloves

Pinch of ground nutmeg
1¼ cups unsweetened oat milk
1 teaspoon pure vanilla extract
2 to 3 tablespoons pure maple syrup, to taste

1. In a blender, combine the beet powder, cinnamon, ginger, cloves, and nutmeg and set aside.

2. In a small saucepan, warm the milk and vanilla over medium heat until the mixture begins to simmer. Remove from the heat.

3. Pour 1 cup of the milk mixture into the blender with the beet powder and spices and blend until smooth, about 1 minute. Pour into a mug.

4. Use a milk frother on the remaining milk or blend on high speed until it gets foamy. Gently pour the foamed milk into the mug over the beet latte and stir with a spoon.

MATCHA THOMAS LATTE

MAKES 1 SERVING

This is the matcha latte recipe that got me hooked on matcha. It's so incredible that it literally sparked the creation of a matcha-dedicated Instagram account (I'm not lying—go follow @matchathomas)! Matcha is a fantastic source of natural, slow-releasing energy without the anxiety or jitters that come with other sources of caffeine. It also aids in concentration, so I love having a cup or two throughout a really busy work day if I can! Add coconut butter and Bulletproof Brain Octane Oil for healthy fats, a metabolism boost, and more brain fuel.

HOT LATTE

½ cup plant milk (I love using oat)
1 teaspoon matcha powder
1 tablespoon pure maple syrup
1 teaspoon pure vanilla extract

1 tablespoon coconut butter (optional)
1 teaspoon Bulletproof Brain Octane Oil (optional)

1. In a small saucepan, combine ¼ cup water and the milk and warm over medium heat until the mixture begins to simmer. Pour it into a blender.

2. Add the matcha powder, maple syrup, vanilla, coconut butter (if using), and Brain Octane Oil (if using) and blend until smooth, about 1 minute. Pour into a mug and enjoy!

ICED LATTE

¾ cup cold plant milk (I love using oat milk)
1 teaspoon matcha powder
1 tablespoon pure maple syrup
1 teaspoon pure vanilla extract

1 teaspoon Bulletproof Brain Octane Oil (optional)
½ cup crushed ice

In a blender, combine all the ingredients and blend until smooth. Pour into a mug and enjoy!

Acknowledgments

"We did it!!! *insert intense fist-pumping here* I still can't believe it. Writing a book is incredibly challenging yet indescribably fulfilling. When I started taking an interest in nutrition as a ten-year-old kid, I never expected it to completely change my life. But through *allll* the crazy challenges and breathtaking moments, it has helped me become someone I'm genuinely proud of, and I'm so grateful for that.

Thank you to my offline and online community and fans. You've unconditionally supported my personal and professional growth over the years, and I'm crazy grateful! Thank you for listening to me, laughing with me, reaching me, debating with me, providing platforms and opportunities for me, and most important, spreading so much love to me and others in our community. You all have shown me the power of connection, regardless of age, gender, religion, race, and so many other perceived barriers. Thank you all for being the inspiration and part of the foundation of my life purpose. Thriving together will always and forever be my biggest motivation.

None of this would have been possible without my parents, Charmaine and Hugh, who have always deeply supported me in creating a life that is uniquely my own. Thank you for empowering little Haile and letting her know her voice, opinions, and ideas matter and should be shared with the world. And thank you for being vulnerable, real humans, who just happened to become parents, for not pretending to be infallible. Seeing you both grow through so many challenges, and even growing through some with me, has been invaluable. I love you endlessly, parental unit!

To my little sister, Nia: Where do I even start? You are the most precious, beautiful soul. You never cease to bring me so much comfort and joy in times when I need it most. You are the built-in best friend of my dreams, and I am eternally grateful for your presence in my life! Thank you for the best memories, inside jokes, and for always encouraging me to lighten up, have fun, and just be me. I love you, angel potato baby!!

Thank you to my siblings, Maleke, Shardiney, Octavia, Alexis, and TJ, and to Uncle Leslie, Aunty Fay, Terrell, Adrian, Joey, Jyzelle, Andrea, Patti, Hannah, and Micaluna, for being the ultimate taste testers and providing encouragement and love as I've grown up over the years.

In no particular order, a massive thank-you to the extraordinary humans and organizations that have been great mentors and friends, taking a chance on me in the various stages throughout my journey: the Alliance for a Healthier Generation team, Megan Corey, Lizzeth Sanchez, Kelly Fryer, Leanne Hernandez, Norma Gentry, Nancy Mehagian, Judy Proffer, Quynn Red Mountain, Susan Santiago, Susan Terry, Hyatt Hotels, Sam Kass, Michelle Obama, Deepak Chopra, Chelsea Clinton, Rachael Ray, Tanya Steel, Eric and Richard Carr, Renee Kreager, Kim-Julie Hansen, the Instagram team, Christen Nino De Guzman, Sheila Sorensen, Gayle Gergely, Dani Nierenberg, Bernie Pollack, Lisa Mayer, Sanah Jivani, the team at Experience Life magazine, former Surgeon General Richard Carmona, Jennifer Cabe, the Canyon Ranch Institute team, Tony Hillary—Gene Baur, Suzanne Pender, and Samantha Pachirat from Farm Sanctuary, Phoebe and Susie from Pine Hill Farm, Elizabeth Sparks, Natalie Barnes Shepp, and Leza Carter from Tucson Village Farm, Chris and the Nature's Pantry New Windsor team, Kathryn and David Thomas from Living Whole. Without the experiences and opportunities you all have made possible, this journey and book would have never blossomed into what they are today. Thank you for helping me strengthen my leadership skills, confidence, and passions.

And a special shout-out to the lovely students and teachers I've worked with all around the world, the people who have challenged me and showed me my strength, and all the media outlets and publications that have created space for me to share my story and message.

I am immensely grateful for the mysterious and beautiful thing that is the universe for bringing the most incredible agency and not-so-secret agents into my life. Sally Ekus, Sara Pokorny, Jaimee Constantine, and Lisa Ekus, thank you. I am ridiculously lucky to work with strong, creative, kind, and passionate women every day. You all continue to teach me how to recognize my worth, fight for my creativity and authenticity to be appreciated, and continue to work with the best intentions. And thank you, Sally, for sending pictures of baby Maybelline as the cutest pick-me-up during this book-writing process!

Thank you to my publisher, William Morrow/HarperCollins, and editors Cassie Jones and Jill Zimmerman, for believing in me and this book. Your support and guidance on this journey have been incredible and surreal. You've both provided so much opportunity for me to deeply grow and get to know myself as a writer. It has been a dream come true working together. And thanks to my terrific team at HQ/HarperCollins in the UK, Kate Fox and Lisa Milton, for all the support from across the pond!

To the Lively Squad, who helped make this book so meaningful and real: thank you for your daily work to make the world a better place. Thank you for shining your light and helping others shine theirs, too. I deeply admire your journeys, vulnerability, talents, and passions, and how you all so authentically connect with yourselves and find ways to connect with and uplift others. Love you, Maya, Hannah, Gabrielle, Lulu, and Nia (and their incredibly loving and uplifting mothers, Deidre, Farida, Marcella, and Holly)!

Thank you to my amazing makeup artist, Chadd Bell. It has been such a joy working with you over the years—you are such a beautiful person inside and out (and the only person in the world I trust with my eyebrows)! As someone who doesn't love makeup, you make me feel confident, vibrant, and most important, like myself. Through all the awesome glam moments we've had, I've always felt like my personality and energy were beautifully expressed through your work. Thank you for helping the Lively Squad express their individuality during the Living Lively shoot!

Thank you to my home slice, Alexsey Reyes, for being so open, flexible, and creative during our lifestyle shoots! You are ridiculously talented, and it was an honor getting to work with you on this. Thank you, Will Coleman, for your commitment and excitement to help make the food photography in this book beautiful and unique, and make the shoot process smooth, organized, and hilarious! Your contribution was invaluable. It still *blows my mind* that we're all under twenty-one and created this book. Gen Z showed up and showed out! I think we did pretty well for our first rodeo, y'all!

To the brands who gifted us with the best snacks, drinks, goodies, and gifts during our photo shoot weekend—I deeply appreciate your support of our work and this book! Thank you:

Sweetgreen
SeaSnax
Blossom Water
Brew Dr Kombucha
Impossible Foods
Q Drinks
Erin Bakers
Jem Organics
Pixie Mood
Snow Monkey
Raised Gluten-Free
Bada Bean Snacks

And finally, thank you to my ancestors. Your persistence and fight to succeed and thrive in the world are the reason I'm here today, and the reason I will continue to ensure that I design a life of meaning, lifting up others along the way. Thank you for your sacrifice and commitment to future generations. I hope I'm what you dreamed of.

Index

Note: Page references in *italics* indicate recipe photographs.

HarperCollins books may be purchased for educational, business, or sales promotional use. For information, please email the Special Markets Department at SPsales@harpercollins.com.

FIRST EDITION

DESIGNED BY RENATA DE OLIVEIRA
LIFESTYLE PHOTOGRAPHY BY ALEXSEY REYES
FOOD PHOTOGRAPHY BY HAILE THOMAS AND WILL COLEMAN
PHOTOGRAPHS OF LUISA GAFFGA BY STEFAN NULLMANN (PAGES 40 AND 41)
ILLUSTRATIONS BY BYELVINA GAFAROVA, ASTARINA, VICTORIA MOROZOVA,
BOSOTOCHKA, and PA3X/SHUTTERSTOCK

Library of Congress Cataloging-in-Publication Data
Names: Thomas, Haile, author.
  Title: Living lively : 80 plant-based recipes to activate your power and feed your potential / Haile Thomas.
Description: New York : William Morrow, 2020. | Includes index. | Summary: "By a superstar eighteen-year-old activist and motivational speaker, and the youngest Certified Integrative Health Coach in America, an inspiring plant-based cookbook featuring 80 delicious, wholesome recipes to boost confidence, happiness, energy, and positivity along with "7 points of power" to motivate the next generation of leaders"—Provided by publisher.
Identifiers: LCCN 2019054725 | ISBN 9780062943415 (hardcover) | ISBN 9780062943422 (ebook)
Subjects: LCSH: Vegetarian cooking. | Cooking (Natural foods) | Health. | LCGFT: Cookbooks.
Classification: LCC TX837 .T4637 2020 | DDC 641.5/636--dc23
LC record available at https://lccn.loc.gov/2019054725

ISBN 978-0-06-294341-5

20 21 22 23 24   LSC   10 9 8 7 6 5 4 3 2 1